The All-American POTATO COOKBOOK

A Benjamin b Company Book

Chief Home Economist: Betty Sullivan
Consulting Home Economists: Carol Peterson, Alice Pearson
Food Technician: Paul Pressman
Editor: Julie Hogan
Editorial Assistants: Susan A. Jablonski, Virginia Schomp, Greta Ebel
Project Manager: David R. Dumke
Art & Design: Thomas C. Brecklin
Typography: A-Line, Milwaukee
Photography: Teri Sandison, Los Angeles

Merchandise courtesy Bullock's Home Store, Bullock's
Beverly Center, Los Angeles

Copyright © 1982 WPGA, Inc. All rights reserved.

Copies of this book are available at discounts in bulk quantities for fund raising, premium, consumer education, and similar programs. Write the publisher for details and costs.

Prepared and published by The Benjamin Company, Inc.
One Westchester Plaza
Elmsford, New York 10523

ISBN: 0-87502-106-9
Library of Congress Catalog Card Number: 82-072354

9 8 7 6 5 4 3 2 1

Table of Contents

I	**The 8th Wonder of the World**	5
	The legend and lore of potatoes. Nutritive values. Buying and storing.	
II	**The Classics**	13
	Basic baked, boiled, fried potatoes of all kinds. Purely potatoes: no additives!	
III	**This Spud's for You!**	23
	Appetizers and snacks, with the emphasis on party foods.	
IV	**The Hot and Cold of It**	33
	A super collection of special soups, chowders, and salads of all kinds.	
V	**Dinner's On the Table**	49
	Meat, seafood, and vegetarian main dishes. Some traditional favorites with many new twists.	
VI	**Humpty Dumpling and Friends**	67
	Yes, dumplings, pancakes, potato noodles, all kinds of side dishes.	
VII	**The Meal in a Peel**	85
	An array of toppings for breakfasts, lunches, dinners, or snacks and so easy!	
VIII	**From the Other Field**	97
	Potatoes are coupled with grains for a solid collection of breads, rolls, and muffins.	
IX	**Not Only From Ireland**	117
	The most popular potato dishes from France, Germany, Greece, Israel, and other countries.	
X	**One Potato-Two Potato-Three Potato-Four**	131
	Fun things to make: pretzels, potato baskets, cookies, candies, etc.	
XI	**When Time is Short**	143
	Those wonderful canned, frozen, and freeze-dried friends and how to make them special.	
XII	**Encore!**	151
	Ideas for storing and recipes that use leftovers.	
	Index	157

The 8th Wonder of the World

The potato. The spud. It's fat-free, tasty, and nutritious. The incredible potato has finally arrived after being attacked, misunderstood and neglected for centuries.

The Quechua Indians of Peru called it "papa" before Spanish explorers christened it "patata" in the 16th century. With more nutrition than soybeans, less calories than a cup of yogurt, and yielding nearly twice as much food per acre as grain, the potato has come a long way from its roots in the Andes Mountains.

But it's not been all that easy. It took over two centuries for potatoes to become accepted in Europe. It's told that Britain's Queen Elizabeth I dismissed a royal chef because no one told him what part of the plant was edible. He served her the leaves! In France, Marie Antoinette helped make potatoes fashionable by wearing potato blossoms in her hair. The French, though, probably understood more about the destiny of potatoes than anyone. They named them "les pommes de terre," literally, "the apples of the earth." Had Eve looked down instead of up, Adam may have been tripped up by a potato!

Louis XVI of France even went so far as to wear potato flowers in his buttonhole to encourage the growing of potatoes. Finally, when an armed guard was assigned to watch the royal potato patch, potatoes were on their way. Today, Europe and Russia account for 75 percent of the world's potato crop. Not bad, especially when you consider that something between 11 billion and 12 billion bushels are grown worldwide each year! Significant? You bet it is: the annual crop is said to be worth more than $106 billion.

The basic types of potatoes (page 6), potato starch flour, dehydrated potato flakes

Spud Comes to the U.S.

Pizarro, the Spanish conqueror of Peru, is believed to have brought the first potato plants to Europe around the middle of the 16th century. In North America, the sweet potato was known to the Indians but it wasn't until the 1620's that the white potato was brought to Virginia from England. Londonderry, New Hampshire, however, gets credit for the true "birth" of the potato in the United States. Irish settlers brought potatoes with them when they settled in Londonderry in 1719. Potatoes were so important to the Irish diet that they came to be known as "Irish" potatoes to distinguish them from sweet potatoes.

While Russia, China, and Poland lead the United States in annual potato production, the U.S. does account for 5 percent of the world's crop. Potatoes are grown commercially in every state.

Versatility

Sure, you can boil them, bake them, mash them, and fry them. Processed products such as frozen fries, chips, canned, and dehydrated potatoes are common. The potato is put to many more uses, however. There's potato starch flour and the potato is the source for vodka and aquavit. We might even find potatoes contributing solutions to our energy problems in the future. Research to convert potatoes into automobile fuel is already well along. Finally, in Europe, potatoes are an extremely important feed for livestock. The 8th Wonder of the World? A fair claim, you bet.

The Harvest

There are four basic types of potatoes and numerous varieties. The types: ☐ The *Round Whites*, available year long, are best for boiling, mashed potatoes, and potato salads. ☐ The *Round Reds*, generally a more moist potato, lend themselves to American Fries, Hash Browns, and potato salads. ☐ The *Long Whites* are also a cooking potato. ☐ But the most outstanding potato today is the oblong-shaped *Russet*, which captures almost 40 percent of all sales and is the classic baked potato and best choice for French fries.

Small "new" potatoes are not a variety, but simply potatoes that are harvested before they reach maximum size and are not placed in storage. They are available year-round in limited quantities. New potatoes are delicious cooked simply in their skins and buttered, or as the star of any type of potato salad.

The recipes in this book all work with any type of potato you prefer. But you will find that, as in all cooking, using different varieties can add meal appeal. Round White, Russet, Round Red, Long White; take your pick and enjoy!

Buying

Potatoes should be fairly clean, firm, and smooth. Choose those with regular shapes so there won't be too much waste in peeling. Potatoes of uniform size will provide even cooking.

Avoid potatoes that are wrinkled, have wilted skins, soft dark areas, cut surfaces, or a green appearance. (Call such produce errors to the attention of the store manager. Demand fresh potatoes! Many stores simply do not store potatoes properly.) US No. 1 is the grade generally available and there are varying sizes within the grade.

Storing

Store potatoes in a cool, humid (but not wet), dark place that's well ventilated. The ideal temperatures are 45°F to 50°F. At that temperature range, potatoes will keep well for a month or two. At temperatures much over that, potatoes should not be stored for more than one week. Warmer temperatures encourage sprouting and shriveling. (Sprouting potatoes can still be used. Just break off the sprouts.)

Avoid prolonged exposure to light which causes potatoes to turn green. This greening causes a bitter flavor so it should be removed before the potato is cooked.

Don't refrigerate potatoes. Below 40°F potatoes develop a sweet taste, the result of an accumulation of sugar in the tubers. This increased sugar will cause the potato to darken when cooked.

Home Freezing of Potatoes

Because of the wide variety, high quality and economy of processed potato products and the year-round availability of fresh potatoes, most people don't find it practical to can or freeze fresh potatoes at home. However, here are some recommendations:

- The best potatoes for freezing are those that have been precooked, such as mashed potato patties, baked stuffed potatoes, or French fries.
- Raw potatoes or potatoes in combination dishes such as soups and stews do not freeze well. Upon thawing and reheating, they tend to disintegrate. If preparing a combination dish for freezing, omit the potatoes and add them during the thawing/reheating step.
- To freeze baked stuffed potatoes or mashed potato patties: Prepare them according to your favorite recipe. Cool quickly in the refrigerator, then freezer-wrap in moisture and vaporproof packaging. Seal, label, date, and freeze. Recommended maximum storage time is one month at 0°F. To serve: Unwrap and reheat at 350°F.
- To freeze homemade French fries: Prepare potatoes as for French Fries (page 20). Precook using the oven or oil methods.

   Oven Method: Arrange potato strips in shallow baking pan, brush with melted butter or margarine, and bake at 450°F just until strips begin to brown, turning occasionally. Cool quickly in refrigerator.

   Oil Method: Blanch potato strips in vegetable oil heated to 370°F until tender but not brown. Drain and cool quickly in refrigerator.

   Place prepared strips in moisture and vaporproof containers or bags. Seal, label, date, and freeze. Recommended maximum storage time is two months at 0°F. To serve using the Oven Method: Return frozen potatoes to baking sheet and bake at 450°F until golden brown, turning occasionally. Or use the Oil Method: Deep-fat fry frozen potatoes at 390°F until golden and crisp.

Potato Equivalents and Substitutions

Fresh Potatoes
1 pound potatoes equals:
- about 3 medium potatoes
- 3 cups peeled and sliced
- 2 1/2 cups peeled and diced
- 2 cups mashed
- 2 cups French fried

Tips on Storing Peeled Potatoes
- Potatoes darken if not cooked soon after they are peeled. To help keep them white, toss with an ascorbic acid mixture or a little lemon juice.
- Do not soak potatoes for prolonged periods. Soaking causes loss of vitamins.

THE RAW TRUTH

The fat-free potato is a nutrient-dense food. It provides good nutritional return for the calories. Why is nutrient density important? Our need for calories has probably decreased by one-third since the turn of the century because we aren't as active. But, in general, we still need about the same amount of nutrients as we did then. This means that in order to get all the nutrition we need without consuming too many calories, we must include many nutrient-dense foods like potatoes in our diet.

Why the Fattening Image?

All too often the potato is guilty by illusion and by association. Although the potato appears to be a bulky vegetable, it is actually 80 percent water, just a little less than is in milk. And its association with high-calorie toppings like butter, sour cream, gravy, and mayonnaise dressing, puts the low-calorie potato at a disadvantage. Just one tablespoon of butter will double the number of calories in a baked potato. There are many low-calorie ways to prepare potatoes deliciously. Here are just a few tasty lower/no calories accompaniments:

- Toasted sesame seeds
- Whipped butter and poppy seed
- A spoonful of stewed tomatoes and a bit of grated cheese
- Melted butter or margarine thinned with lemon juice
- A mix of dried herbs: parsley, chives, basil, dill
- Mock Sour Cream (page 80)
- Chopped onion with coarsely grated black pepper
- Chive-spiked yogurt

A Word About Calories

The best diet is one based on a variety of nutritious foods. And the potato offers a high return of nutrients for relatively few calories. Many people think they know which foods are high in calories and which are low in calories. But a direct comparison between the following foods, many of which are generally included on weight control diets, may surprise you.

FOOD COMPARISONS

Food	Serving Size	Calories*
The Potato		
Baked	1 medium (150 grams)	100
Boiled	1 medium (150 grams)	100
Chips	10 regular or ridged	110
French-fried	10 2 to 3 1/2-inch pieces	110
Mashed with milk	3/4 cup	100**
Apple	1 medium (150 grams)	80
Cottage Cheese, creamed	1/2 cup	130
Hamburger pattie	3 ounces cooked	270
Lettuce salad with Italian dressing	1 cup with 2 tablespoons dressing	170
Low-fat milk	1 cup	150
Noodles	1 cup	200
Orange juice	1 cup	110
Rice	3/4 cup	170
Spaghetti	1 cup	160
White bread	1 slice	70
Yogurt, plain	1 cup	120

* Source: Values based on "Nutrition Labeling, Tools for Its Use," USDA Agriculture Information Bulletin No. 382. All calories rounded up to the nearest 10, as called for in FDA labeling regulations.

** Source: Value based on "Composition of Foods," USDA Agriculture Handbook No. 8.

Vitamins and Minerals

The potato gives us a wide spectrum of valuable nutrients. For example, it is one of our most important sources of complex carbohydrates, often lacking in the American diet.

The potato is a good source of vitamins C and B_6, and has long been known to be a storehouse of minerals, such as manganese, chromium, selenium, and potassium. It is an especially good source for iron.

One current nutritional goal is to reduce the amount of sodium consumed. A typical potato provides less than 10mg. of sodium — compared to an average typical daily intake of more than 4,000mg.

Fiber

Fiber has been the subject of renewed interest. It is that part of the food we eat that is not digested by the body but travels through and holds water, forming the bulk we need for eliminating solid waste. While official recommendations for fiber haven't been established, about six grams daily is considered desirable, and most of us fall short of this amount. Potatoes can add to overall fiber intake. An average serving provides about 10 percent of a desirable daily intake of fiber.

Carbohydrates

Carbohydrates are the body's primary source of fuel for energy. Furthermore, carbohydrates are not especially fattening, as is commonly thought. Gram for gram, fats are more than twice as fattening as either carbohydrates or proteins. And potatoes are virtually fat-free.

Nutrition in a Raw Potato

Nutrient	Value in Medium Potato (150 grams)	Percent of U.S. RDA (Est. 1973)
Calories	100	
Fat	0g	
Carbohydrates	22g	
Vitamin A	Trace	
Vitamin C	21.43mg	35%
Thiamin	.061mg	4%
Riboflavin (B_2)	.049mg	2%
Niacin	1.76mg	10%
Calcium	14mg	—
Iron	2.7mg	10%
Vitamin B_6	.352mg	20%
Folic Acid	29.8mg	8%
Phosphorus	78.31mg	8%
Magnesium	29.7mg	8%
Zinc	.524mg	4%
Copper	.245mg	10%
Iodine	.035mg	15%

To calculate nutritional value of a 250-gram potato (a typical baking potato) multiply values given by 1.6.

Source: Potato Market Basket Study 1978-79 to establish nutritional labeling under Food and Drug Administration regulations.

The Classics

Childhood memories bring back Sunday dinners with gloriously mashed potatoes (and Grandma's chicken, of course). Yet, the potato at its most basic can be so many different things. Presented here are the potato classics — no-frills preparation of the pure vegetable itself.

Mashed Potatoes — 6 servings

- 5 large potatoes, washed and peeled
- 1 tablespoon salt
- 1 cup milk
- 6 tablespoons butter or margarine
- Butter (optional)
- Paprika (optional)

Cut potatoes into quarters. Bring 1 inch water and salt to a boil in large saucepan. Add potatoes. Cover and boil 20 minutes, or until tender. Drain thoroughly. Let stand, uncovered. In small saucepan, heat milk and butter until butter melts. Do not boil. Remove from heat. Mash potatoes with potato masher, fork, or electric mixer until smooth and no lumps remain. Gradually beat in milk mixture; beat until creamy and fluffy. Spoon potatoes into warm serving bowl. Top with a pat of butter or margarine and sprinkle with paprika, if desired. Garnish with minced parsley, chives, watercress, or mint.

For lower calorie mashed potatoes, substitute skim milk for whole milk. Do not add butter.

Basic Baked Potatoes ———————————— 1 serving

1 or more large potatoes
 (6 to 8 ounces)

Preheat oven to 400°F. Scrub potatoes with brush in cold water; rinse well; dry with paper towels. For soft skins, rub with shortening or wrap in aluminum foil. For crisp skins, dry thoroughly. Pierce potatoes with fork. Place potatoes on oven rack or baking sheet. Bake 45 to 60 minutes, or until potatoes are easily pierced with fork. For perfect baked potatoes, gently roll back and forth on flat surface before serving. To serve, cut a cross in top of each potato; pinch to open. Top with any of the following: 1 tablespoon dairy sour cream, chopped chives, parsley, green onion, grated Parmesan cheese, or crumbled, crisp bacon.

Potatoes of uniform size will cook in the same length of time.

Baked in Coals: Scrub and rinse potatoes. Pierce potatoes with fork. Bury potatoes, unwrapped or wrapped in aluminum foil, in hot coals 45 to 60 minutes, or until easily pierced with fork. Skins will be black.

Baked on the Grill: Scrub and rinse potatoes. Pierce potatoes with fork. Place on grill. Cook about 60 minutes, or until easily pierced with fork.

Microwave Instructions: Scrub and rinse potatoes. Pierce potatoes with fork. Place 1 inch apart in spoke-fashion on microwave rack. Cook on High, turning potatoes over halfway through cooking time. Let stand 3 minutes before serving.

Cooking Time*

1 potato (6 to 8 ounces) 4 to 6 minutes
2 potatoes (6 to 8 ounces each) 6 to 8 minutes
3 potatoes (6 to 8 ounces each) 8 to 12 minutes
4 potatoes (6 to 8 ounces each) 12 to 16 minutes

*Cooking time calculated for 600 watt microwave oven. If using 400 watt oven, cook one-third longer than times provided.

Roasted Potato Fans ——————— 6 servings

    6 medium potatoes, washed and peeled
    6 tablespoons butter or margarine
    1/2 teaspoon salt
    1/4 teaspoon basil
    1/4 teaspoon marjoram
    1/8 teaspoon pepper

Cut potatoes vertically into 1/4-inch thick slices, cutting each slice only 3/4 of the way through the potato. Preheat oven to 400°F. Place butter in 9 × 13-inch baking dish. Place baking dish in oven to melt butter. Arrange potatoes, cut-side up, in baking dish; brush on melted butter. Sprinkle with salt, basil, marjoram, and pepper. Bake 1 hour, or until slices are fanned out and golden brown. Brush occasionally with butter in baking dish.

Boiled Potatoes ——————— 4 to 6 servings

    4 large or 6 medium potatoes, washed and peeled
    1/2 teaspoon salt

Cut potatoes into quarters. Bring 1 quart water and salt to a boil in large saucepan. Add potatoes. Cover and boil 20 to 30 minutes, or until tender. Drain thoroughly. (Reserve potato water for other uses, such as soup.) For perfect boiled potatoes, place a folded towel over saucepan; let stand 5 minutes. Shake pan. Remove towel. Turn into warm serving bowl.

You can pressure-cook large, whole potatoes at 15 pounds for 15 minutes. If potatoes are cut up, pressure-cook at 15 pounds for 2 1/2 minutes.

Steakhouse Fries ——————— 6 servings

    6 large potatoes, washed and peeled
    Peanut or corn oil for deep-fat frying
    Salt (optional)

Follow directions for French Fries (page 20), cutting potatoes into 3/4 × 1/4-inch strips. Dry thoroughly on paper towels before deep frying. Sprinkle with salt before serving, if desired.

Parslied Small Potatoes ——— 3 to 4 servings

1 pound small potatoes, washed; do not peel
3 tablespoons butter or margarine
1 tablespoon minced parsley
1/2 teaspoon paprika
1/4 teaspoon salt

Bring 1 inch water to a boil in large saucepan. Add potatoes; cover and boil 10 minutes, or until tender; drain. Peel potatoes by holding each with a fork and peeling with paring knife. Place whole potatoes in warm serving bowl. Melt butter in small saucepan. Stir parsley, paprika, and salt into butter. Pour butter mixture over potatoes. Serve immediately.

To save some time, you can boil potatoes and drain as above. Do not peel potatoes. Add melted butter to potatoes in saucepan. Shake saucepan to coat potatoes with butter.

You can also pressure-cook small potatoes at 15 pounds about 2 1/2 minutes.

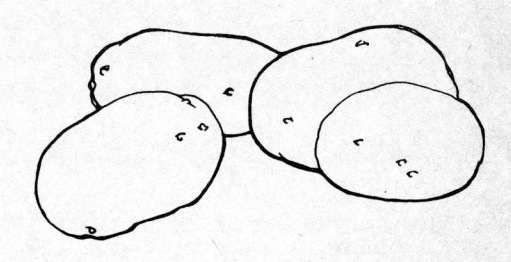

Steamed Potatoes ——— 4 servings

4 medium potatoes, washed, peeled or unpeeled

Place wire rack in kettle of large saucepan. Add water to just below level of rack. Bring water to a boil. Add potatoes, cover tightly, and steam until tender. Whole potatoes will take 30 to 45 minutes. Cut-up potatoes will take 20 to 30 minutes. Check occasionally to see if additional water is needed.

If you do not have a rack, use inverted custard cups or crumpled aluminum foil to elevate potatoes.

Twice-Baked Potatoes — 6 servings

- 6 large, Basic Baked Potatoes (page 14), hot
- 3 to 4 tablespoons butter or margarine
- 1/3 cup milk or light cream, heated
- 1 teaspoon onion powder
- 1 teaspoon salt
- 1/8 teaspoon white pepper
- 2 egg whites
- 1/2 cup grated Swiss or Cheddar cheese
- Paprika

Cut potatoes in half crosswise; carefully scoop out pulp, leaving a 1/4-inch shell. Or, for larger shells, cut down through top of potato, removing only a small portion of top; carefully remove pulp. Place pulp in mixing bowl. Add butter, milk, onion powder, salt, and pepper. Beat with electric mixer until smooth; set aside. In small bowl, beat egg whites until stiff peaks form. Fold egg whites into potato mixture. Preheat oven to 400°F. Fill potato shells. Sprinkle with cheese and paprika. Bake for 10 minutes, or until cheese is melted.

Sour Cream Twice-Baked Potatoes

Combine 1 envelope (1 1/2 ounces) sour cream mix, 3/4 cup milk, salt, pepper, 1/2 teaspoon cumin, and 1 teaspoon butter in small bowl; blend well. Stir into potato pulp; blend well. Fill potato shells. Sprinkle with paprika. Bake as above.

Cheese-Stuffed Twice-Baked Potatoes

Combine 1/2 cup milk and 1/4 cup butter in small saucepan; heat until butter melts, stirring constantly. Stir into potato pulp. Add 1/2 cup sour cream, 1/2 cup cubed Swiss cheese, salt and pepper to taste. Fill shells. Bake at 350°F 25 minutes. Top with 1/4 cup shredded Swiss cheese, divided among potatoes. Return to oven until cheese melts.

Low-Calorie Twice-Baked Potatoes

Combine 2/3 cup hot water, 6 tablespoons nonfat dry milk powder, 1 tablespoon imitation butter, salt, and pepper in small bowl. Stir into potato pulp. Beat until fluffy and smooth. Fill shells. Sprinkle with paprika. Bake at 350°F for 20 minutes. This recipe saves about 60 calories per potato.

Potato Chips ———— 4 quarts

8 large potatoes, washed and peeled
Ice water
Peanut or corn oil for deep-fat frying
Salt (optional)

Slice potatoes paper-thin (approximately 1/16") with a vegetable peeler or sharp knife. Soak slices in ice water for 2 hours. Heat oil in deep-fat fryer (or 4 inches oil in large, deep saucepan) to 380°F. Drain potato slices; dry thoroughly on paper towels. Place separated slices in fry basket. Lower into oil. Shake basket or stir several times to prevent slices from sticking together. Deep-fat fry until golden. Remove from oil. Drain well on paper towels. Sprinkle with salt, if desired. Cool before serving. Store in airtight container.

Hash Browns ———— 6 servings

6 medium Basic Baked Potatoes (page 14), bake at least the day before and refrigerate
1/3 cup butter, margarine, bacon fat, or vegetable shortening
1 medium onion, thinly sliced
1 tablespoon parsley flakes
1 teaspoon salt
1/4 teaspoon pepper

Peel potatoes; grate coarsely, shred, or dice (4 cups). Melt butter in heavy 10-inch skillet. Sauté onion until transparent. Add potatoes, parsley, salt, and pepper. Do not pack potatoes down. Cook on moderate heat until golden brown and loosened from pan. Turn and brown other side. Serve hot.

Potato Chips, Hash Browns, French Fries (page 20), Twice-Baked Potatoes (page 17)

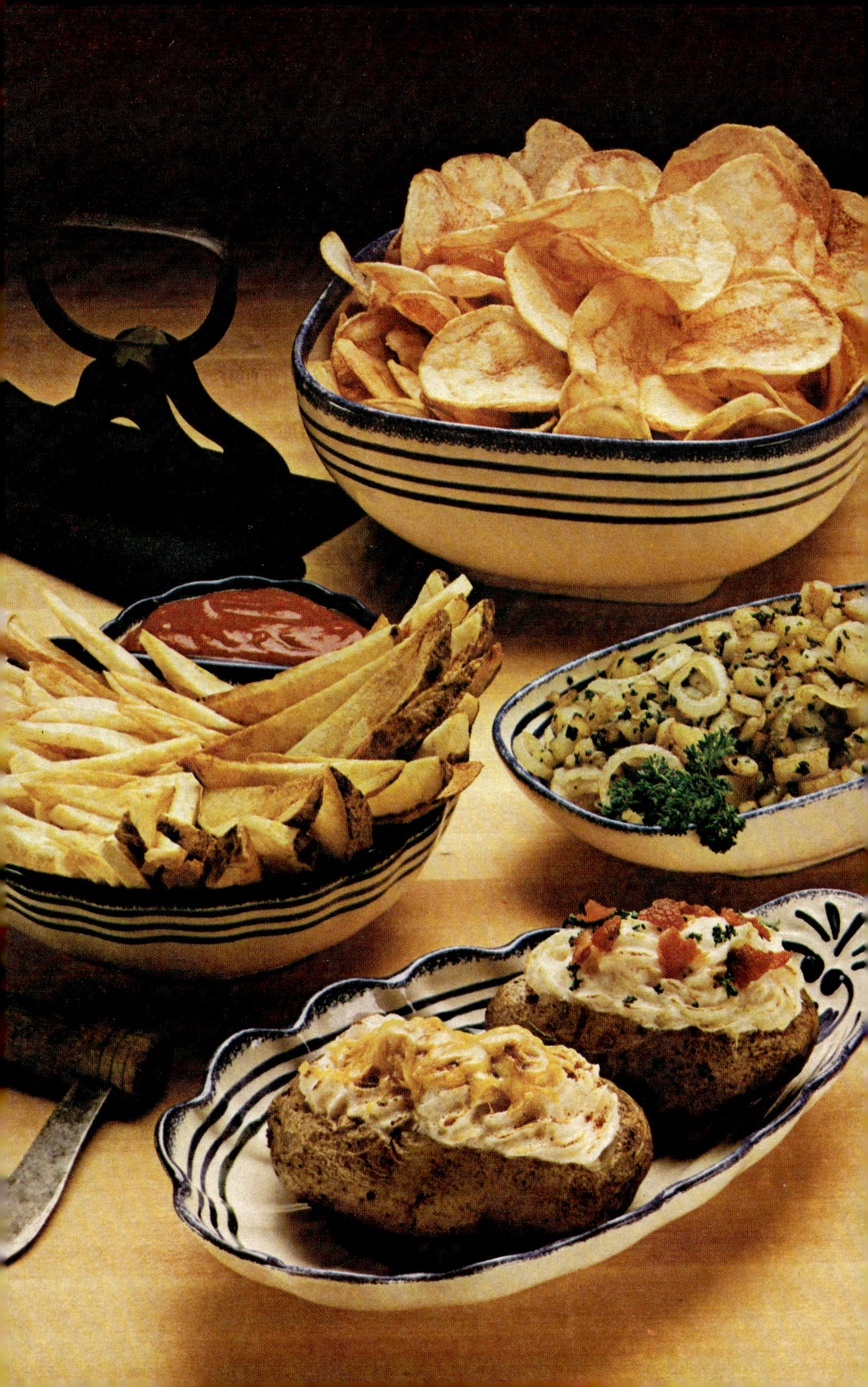

French Fries _____ 6 servings

6 large potatoes, washed and peeled
Ice water
Peanut or corn oil for deep-fat frying
Salt (optional)

Trim sides and ends of potatoes to form blocks. Cut lengthwise into 1/2-inch slices; stack slices evenly. Turn on side; slice again 1/2-inch wide. Soak in ice water for 20 minutes. Heat oil in deep-fat fryer (or 4 inches oil in large, deep saucepan) to 300°F. Drain potatoes; pat dry with paper towels. Place about 1 cup potatoes in fry basket or saucepan. Lower into oil. Deep-fat fry until potatoes are transparent but not browned. Remove basket from oil or use slotted spoon. Drain on paper towels. Just before serving, heat oil to 360°F. Deep fry, 1 cup potatoes at a time, until crisp and golden brown. Drain on paper towels. Sprinkle with salt, if desired. Serve immediately, or can be kept warm in oven.

For lower calorie French Fries, soak potatoes in ice water; drain; dry thoroughly on paper towels. Preheat oven to 450°F. Spread in single layer on jelly-roll pan. Brush with 2 tablespoons vegetable oil. Shake pan to coat potatoes with oil. Bake until tender and golden brown, about 35 minutes. Sprinkle with salt, paprika, and pepper, if desired. Makes 8 servings, about 100 calories per serving.

American Fries _____ 4 to 6 servings

6 medium Boiled Potatoes (page 15), chilled
3 tablespoons butter, margarine, bacon fat, or vegetable shortening
Salt
Pepper

Peel and slice potatoes. Melt butter in large, heavy skillet. Sauté potatoes, without stirring, until golden brown. Turn and brown other side. Sprinkle with salt and pepper.

You can add 2 tablespoons minced onion to potatoes before cooking, if desired.

Potato Puffs ———————————————— 4 servings

    Peanut or corn oil for
      deep-fat frying
    1/2 cup all-purpose flour
    1 teaspoon baking powder
    1/4 teaspoon salt
    1 cup Mashed Potatoes (page 13), at room temperature
    1 egg, slightly beaten
    1 teaspoon minced parsley
    Salt (optional)

Heat oil in deep-fat fryer (or 4 inches oil in large, deep saucepan) to 385°F. Combine flour, baking powder, and salt in medium bowl. Add potatoes; blend thoroughly. Add egg and parsley; blend well. Drop potato mixture by teaspoonfuls into hot oil. Deep-fat fry until golden brown. Remove with slotted spoon. Drain on paper towels. Sprinkle with salt, if desired.

Game Chips ———————————————— 4 servings

    2 large potatoes, washed; do not peel
    Ice water
    Peanut or corn oil for deep-fat frying
    Salt (optional)
    Pepper (optional)

Cut potatoes into 20 sticks. Soak in ice water 2 hours; drain. Dry thoroughly on paper towels. Heat oil in deep-fat fryer (or 4 inches oil in large, deep saucepan) to 375°F. Deep-fat fry, 8 chips at a time, until golden brown. Drain chips on paper towels. Sprinkle with salt and pepper, if desired. Repeat for remaining chips. Serve in basket as dippers.

Shoestring Potatoes ———————————— 6 servings

    6 large potatoes, washed and peeled
    Ice water
    Peanut or corn oil for deep-fat frying
    Salt (optional)

Follow directions for French Fries (page 20), cutting potatoes into 3/16-inch strips. Soak potatoes in ice water 20 minutes. Dry thoroughly on paper towels before deep-fat frying. Sprinkle with salt before servings, if desired.

Cottage Fries ——————————————— 4 servings

  4 medium potatoes, washed and peeled
  3 tablespoons butter, margarine, bacon fat, or vegetable shortening
  Salt
  Pepper

Slice potatoes. Melt butter in heavy 10-inch skillet. Add potatoes. Cover and cook on low heat 15 minutes. Remove cover. Increase heat slightly and cook 10 minutes, or until brown and crispy on bottom. Sprinkle with salt and pepper. Serve immediately.

Potatoes can be coarsely grated instead of sliced.

You can add 1 sliced, medium onion to potatoes before cooking, if desired.

Riced Potatoes ——————————————— 6 servings

  6 medium potatoes, washed and peeled
  1/2 teaspoon salt
  2 tablespoons butter or margarine, melted

Cut potatoes in quarters. Bring 1 quart water and salt to a boil in large saucepan. Add potatoes. Cover and boil 20 to 30 minutes, or until tender. Drain thoroughly. (Reserve potato water for other uses, such as soup.) Let stand, uncovered, until dry. Process through food mill or ricer. Spoon into warm serving dish. Pour melted butter over top.

This Spud's for You!

Those attractive bits and nibbles served to put guests at ease and to create a festive spirit are featured here. Versatility and the ability to complement other flavors make the potato a natural as an opening act for any occasion. The only problem with these delectable, eye-appealing appetizers is that you might not have enough. Be sure to make plenty, because the "a-a-a-h's" will have it, demanding more.

Liver Sausage and Potato Ring

30 servings

- 1 package (3 ounces) lemon-flavored gelatin
- 3/4 cup boiling water
- 1 pound liver sausage (Braunschweiger), casing removed
- 2 cups Riced Potatoes (page 22), at room temperature
- 1 can (8 ounces) tomato sauce
- 1 tablespoon vinegar
- 1/2 teaspoon salt
- 2 hard-cooked eggs, sliced

Lightly oil 1-quart ring mold; set aside. In small bowl, dissolve gelatin in boiling water; set aside. Combine liver sausage, potatoes, tomato sauce, vinegar, and salt in large bowl; beat with electric mixer until thoroughly blended. Add gelatin; blend thoroughly. Pour into prepared ring mold. Chill 8 hours. Unmold onto serving platter. Garnish with hard-cooked egg slices. Serve as spread on crackers or cocktail party rye bread.

Spicy Potato Peels ———————— 4 to 6 servings

3 large Basic Baked Potatoes (page 14), hot
1/4 cup butter or margarine, melted
1/2 teaspoon onion juice
1/4 teaspoon Worcestershire sauce
Salt (optional)
Freshly ground pepper (optional)

Cut potatoes in half lengthwise; scoop out pulp, leaving 1/2-inch thick shell. Use knife to cut shells into 1/2-inch strips. Place strips on baking sheet. Combine butter, onion juice, and Worcestershire. Brush on strips. Sprinkle generously with salt and pepper, if desired. Broil 5 inches from heat, 5 to 7 minutes, or until strips are golden brown. Serve warm.

Oriental Dip ———————————————— 2 cups

1 cup mayonnaise
1 can (8 ounces) water chestnuts, drained and finely chopped
1/2 cup dairy sour cream
2 tablespoons soy sauce
1 tablespoon minced onion
1 teaspoon instant beef bouillon granules
Potato Chips (page 18), or Game Chips (page 21)

Combine mayonnaise, water chestnuts, sour cream, soy sauce, onion, and bouillon in large bowl. Beat with electric mixer until thoroughly blended. Chill at least 2 hours. Serve as dip with chips.

Twice-Baked Potato Skins ———— 16 appetizers

8 Basic Baked Potatoes (page 14)
2 tablespoons melted butter
1 teaspoon garlic powder
1/2 cup shredded Cheddar cheese
1/3 cup cooked, crumbled bacon
Dairy sour cream
Minced chives

Preheat oven to 425°F. Cut potatoes in half lengthwise; carefully remove all pulp. Brush insides of potato shells with melted butter. Sprinkle insides with garlic powder. Divide and sprinkle cheese evenly among shells. Sprinkle with bacon. Place on baking sheet. Bake about 10 minutes, or until skins are crisp. Top with sour cream and chives.

Tiffany Chips — 4 to 6 servings

- 3 large potatoes, washed; do not peel
- 1/2 cup catsup
- 1 teaspoon prepared mustard
- 1/2 teaspoon paprika
- 1/4 cup soft bread crumbs

Preheat oven to 425°F. Cut each potato horizontally into 8 equal slices. Arrange potato slices on lightly greased baking sheet; place potato ends cut-side up; set aside. Combine catsup, mustard, and paprika in small bowl; blend well. Brush mixture on potato slices. Sprinkle bread crumbs on each slice. Bake 30 to 35 minutes, or until potatoes are tender. Serve warm.

To prepare in a microwave oven, prepare slices as directed above. Place slices on microproof plate. Cook on High 6 to 8 minutes, or until potatoes are tender. Let stand 3 minutes before serving.

Hawaiian Tidbits — 18 appetizers

- 2 Italian sausages, casings removed, cut into 18 slices
- 1 large potato, washed, peeled, and cut into 18 cubes
- 1 can (5 1/4 ounces) pineapple chunks, drained
- 2 tablespoons teriyaki sauce

Preheat oven to 375°F. Using wooden skewers, alternate 1 piece sausage, 1 cube potato, and 1 chunk pineapple on each skewer. Lay each kabob on lightly greased baking sheet. Brush with teriyaki sauce. Bake 20 to 25 minutes, or until sausage is cooked and potatoes are tender. Turn several times during cooking. Serve hot.

Vegetable Dip — 1 1/4 cups

- 1 cup mayonnaise
- 1 1/2 teaspoons horseradish
- 1 teaspoon onion flakes
- 1 teaspoon curry powder
- 1/4 teaspoon garlic powder
- 1 teaspoon tarragon vinegar
- French Fries (page 20) or Potato Chips (page 18)

Combine mayonnaise, horseradish, onion flakes, curry powder, garlic powder, and vinegar in small bowl. Stir until blended. Refrigerate 2 hours. Serve as dip with French Fries or Potato Chips.

Tangy Crisp Potato Peels

4 to 6 servings

3 large Basic Baked Potatoes (page 14), hot
1/4 cup butter or margarine, melted
5 drops hot pepper sauce
Salt
Freshly ground pepper
Dairy sour cream

Cut potatoes in half lengthwise; carefully remove all pulp. Use scissors to cut potato skins into 2-inch long × 1-inch wide strips. Place potato strips on baking sheet. Combine butter and hot pepper sauce in small dish. Brush on potato strips. Sprinkle with salt and pepper. Broil, 5 inches from heat, 4 to 6 minutes, or until peels are very crisp and brown. Serve warm with sour cream as a dip.

You can deep-fat fry potato strips in 380°F oil about 45 seconds, or until crisp. Drain on paper towels. Sprinkle with seasoned salt or garlic salt.

Nacho Rounds

5 to 6 servings

1 large potato, washed; do not peel
2 tablespoons hot taco sauce
1 can (4 ounces) chopped mild or hot green chilies, drained
3/4 cup shredded Cheddar cheese

Preheat oven to 350°F. Cut potato vertically into 20 slices. Place in single layer on greased baking sheet. Brush each slice with taco sauce. Sprinkle with chilies and cheese. Bake 25 minutes, or until potatoes are tender and cheese is golden brown. Serve warm.

To prepare in a microwave oven, prepare potatoes as directed above. Place half of slices in circle on microproof plate. Cook on High 6 to 8 minutes, or until potatoes are tender. Repeat with remaining slices. Let stand 3 minutes before serving.

Tangy Crisp Potato Peels, Nacho Rounds, Hawaiian Tidbits (page 25)

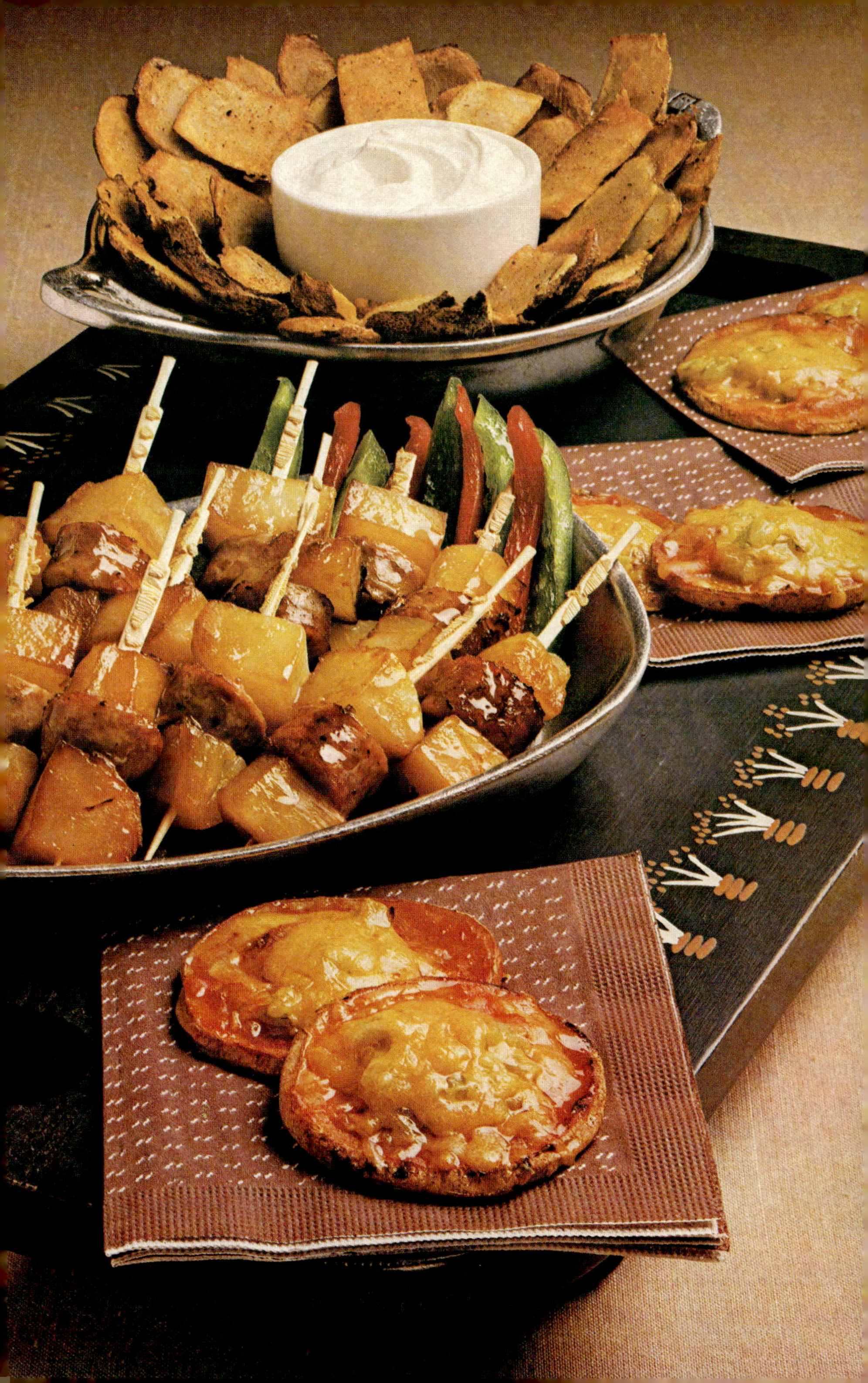

Fried Potato Logs ———————————— 28 appetizers

2 cups Mashed Potatoes (page 13), chilled
1 egg yolk
1 tablespoon onion flakes
1/3 cup all-purpose flour
1 egg
1/2 cup dry bread crumbs
5 tablespoons vegetable shortening

Combine potatoes, egg yolk, and onion flakes in medium bowl; blend well. Shape mixture into 28 logs about 2 1/2 inches long. Roll logs in flour to coat. Combine egg and 2 tablespoons water in small bowl; mix lightly. Dip logs in egg, then into bread crumbs. Melt shortening in large skillet on moderate heat. Fry logs, 8 at a time, until golden brown, turning to brown all sides. Cool slightly before serving.

Potato Cheese Balls ———————— 28 to 30 appetizers

2 cups Mashed Potatoes (page 13), chilled
1/2 cup grated process American cheese
1 egg
1 tablespoon milk
1/2 cup dry bread crumbs

Combine potatoes and cheese in medium bowl; blend well. Shape mixture into 28 to 30 balls. In separate bowl, whisk together egg and milk. Dip balls in egg, then roll in bread crumbs. Place balls on baking sheet. Broil, 5 inches from heat, 4 to 6 minutes, or until golden brown. Turn and brown other side, about 4 minutes. Serve warm on wooden toothpicks.

Crab Meat Slices ———————————— 16 appetizers

1 can (6 1/2 ounces) crab meat drained and picked over
1/4 cup mayonnaise
2 tablespoons dairy sour cream
1 teaspoon minced onion
1 large Basic Baked Potato (page 14)
16 slices cocktail party rye bread

Combine crab meat, mayonnaise, sour cream and onion in small bowl; blend well. Cut potato vertically into 16 slices. Arrange bread slices in a single layer on large serving platter. Top each bread slice with potato slice and 1 tablespoon crab meat mixture. Chill until ready to serve.

Curried Chicken Balls ─────────── 6 to 8 servings

- 1 cup Mashed Potatoes (page 13), chilled
- 1 can (5 ounces) boned chicken
- 1 package (3 ounces) cream cheese, softened
- 1 teaspoon salt
- 1/2 teaspoon curry powder
- 1/2 teaspoon pepper
- 1/2 cup chopped blanched almonds
- 1/2 cup minced parsley

Combine potatoes, chicken, cream cheese, salt, curry powder, and pepper in medium bowl; blend well. Shape into 28 1-inch balls. Combine almonds and parsley in small bowl; mix lightly. Roll each ball in almond-parsley mixture to coat. Arrange on serving tray. Chill at least 2 hours before serving.

Potato Sticks ─────────────── 32 appetizers

- 2 large potatoes; washed; do not peel
- Ice water
- Peanut or corn oil for deep-fat frying
- 1 egg, slightly beaten
- 1/2 cup dry bread crumbs
- 1/4 cup grated Parmesan cheese

Cut each potato into 16 sticks. Soak in ice water 2 hours; drain. Dry thoroughly on paper towels. Heat oil in deep-fat fryer (or 4 inches oil in large, deep saucepan) to 375°F. Dip sticks in egg; then roll in crumbs and cheese. Deep-fat fry, 8 to 10 sticks at a time, until golden brown. Repeat for remaining sticks. Serve as is or as dippers.

Potato Chip Appetizer Dip ─────── 3/4 cup

- 2 packages (3 ounces each) cream cheese, room temperature
- 1 package (4 ounces) blue cheese, room temperature
- 1 tablespoon milk
- 1 tablespoon prepared mustard
- 1 teaspoon onion flakes
- 1/4 teaspoon garlic powder
- 2 to 3 drops hot pepper sauce
- Potato Chips (page 18)

In small mixing bowl, or bowl of food processor fitted with steel blade, combine cream cheese, blue cheese, milk, mustard, onion, garlic powder, and hot pepper sauce; blend well. Chill 1 to 2 hours. Serve as dip with Potato Chips.

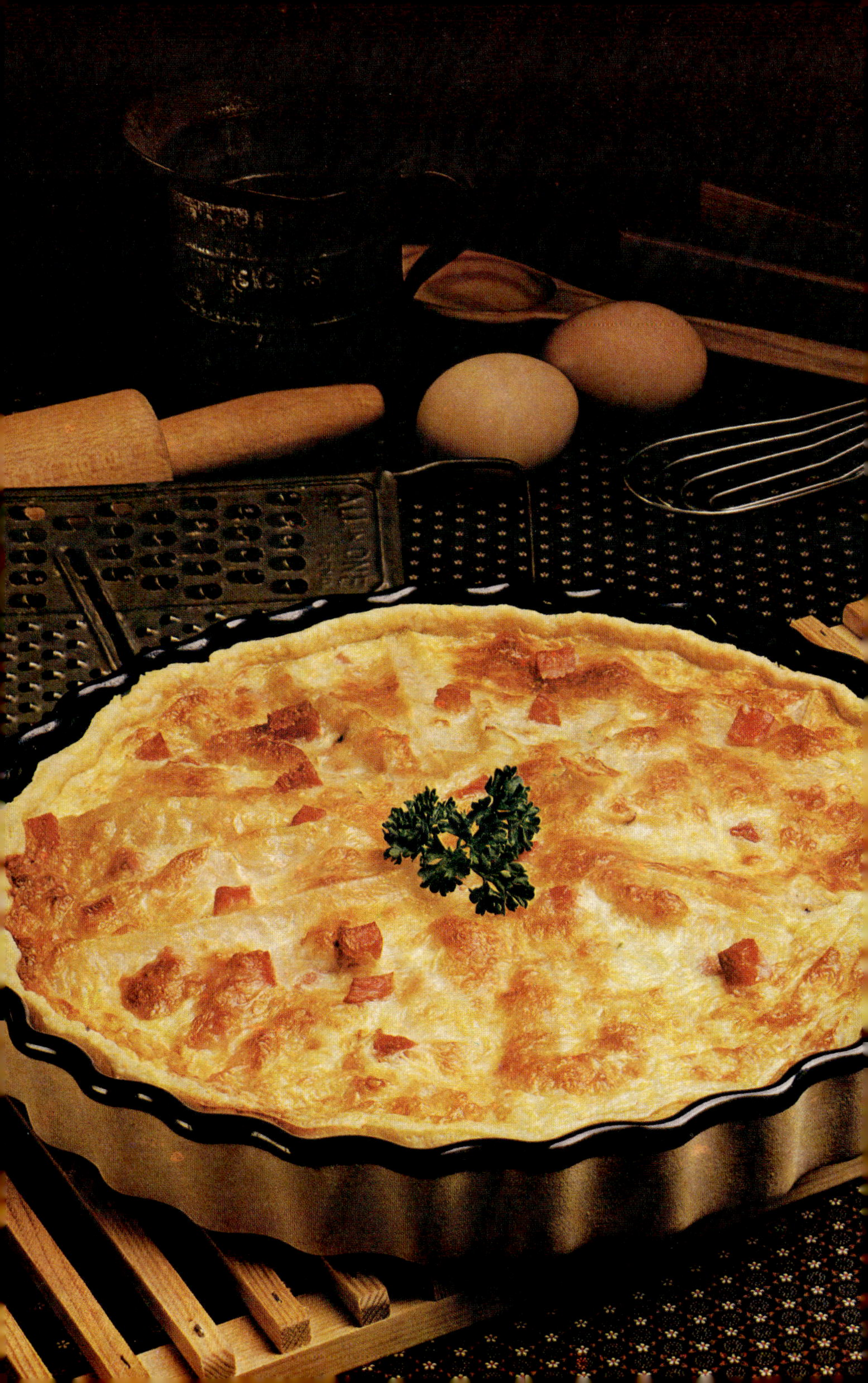

Ham and Potato Quiche ———— 12 servings

- 1 cup all-purpose flour
- 1/2 cup vegetable shortening
- 3/4 teaspoon salt, divided
- 3 to 4 tablespoons cold water
- 1 1/2 cups cubed, cooked ham,
- 1 medium Boiled Potato, peeled and cut (page 15) into 3-inch strips
- 1 cup grated Swiss cheese
- 1 cup milk
- 4 eggs
- 1 teaspoon onion flakes
- 1/4 teaspoon white pepper

Preheat oven to 350°F. Combine flour, shortening, and 1/4 teaspoon salt in large bowl; mix with fork or pastry blender until mixture is consistency of fine crumbs. Gradually add water; stir until dough holds together. Gather dough into a ball. Roll out on lightly floured pastry cloth to a circle 2 inches larger than 9-inch pie plate. Ease crust into pie plate; trim and flute edges. Sprinkle ham, potato, and cheese evenly over bottom of crust. Combine milk, eggs, onion flakes, remaining 1/2 teaspoon salt, and pepper in small bowl; mix lightly. Pour over ingredients in crust. Bake 45 to 50 minutes, or until center is set. Let stand 10 minutes. Slice into 12 wedges.

To prepare in a microwave oven, prepare crust as directed above. Ease into 9-inch glass pie plate; trim and flute edges. Pierce crust with fork. Cook on High 6 to 7 minutes, or until crust is dry and blistered. Prepare filling as directed above, substituting 1 can (13 ounces) undiluted evaporated milk for 1 cup milk. Cook on Medium High 12 to 14 minutes, or until center appears to be set. Cover with aluminum foil. Let stand on heatproof surface 10 minutes. Cut into wedges.

Potato Bread Cordon Bleu ———————————— 9 servings

- 1 loaf unsliced Potato Bread (page 114)
- 1 cup butter or margarine, softened
- 1/8 cup minced chives
- 1 tablespoon lemon juice
- 1 tablespoon prepared mustard
- 2 teaspoons poppy seed
- 3/4 teaspoon grated lemon peel
- 1/4 teaspoon pepper
- 8 slices Swiss cheese
- 8 slices bacon, cooked, drained, and crumbled

Preheat oven to 350°F. Slice bread into 9 pieces, without cutting all the way through bottom crust; set aside. Place butter in medium bowl; beat with electric mixer until fluffy. Add chives, lemon juice, mustard, poppy seed, lemon peel, and pepper; blend well. Remove 3 tablespoons mixture; set aside. Spread remaining mixture on cut surfaces of bread. Place 1 slice cheese between each bread slice. Sprinkle bacon between bread slices. Spread reserved lemon-butter mixture on top and sides of loaf. Bake 15 to 20 minutes, or until loaf is hot. Serve immediately.

Bacon Tater Bits ———————————— 4 to 6 servings

- 24 frozen fried potato tots
- 24 strips (1 × 1 1/2 inches) process American cheese
- 8 slices bacon, cut into thirds

Prepare potato tots according to package directions; cool. Place a strip of cheese on a piece of bacon. Top with a potato tot. Roll up. Secure with wooden toothpicks. Repeat for remaining ingredients. Place on broiler pan. Broil, 5 inches from heat, 8 minutes, or until bacon is crisp, turning once after 4 minutes. Serve hot.

To prepare in a microwave oven, prepare bits as directed above. Place half on paper towel-lined microproof plate. Cover with a paper towel. Cook on High 4 minutes. Turn bits over. Cover and cook on High 3 minutes, or until bacon is thoroughly cooked. Repeat for remaining bits. Let stand 1 minute before serving.

The Hot and Cold of It

A quick glance will show you that this well-rounded collection of superior soups, choice chowders, and select salads lets your affection for the spud run hot and cold. Choose Pumpkin-Potato Soup or the Fish-Potato Chowder on a wintry day. Madison Avenue Potato Salad or Superb Garden Salad for a poolside party. Come on in. The weather's fine and you'll love the extremes.

Ham and Potato Chowder — 6 servings

- 2 tablespoons butter or margarine
- 1/4 cup chopped onion
- 1/4 cup chopped green pepper
- 4 medium potatoes, washed, peeled, and cubed (3 cups)
- 1 teaspoon salt
- 1/4 teaspoon paprika
- 1/8 teaspoon pepper
- 3 tablespoons all-purpose flour
- 2 cups milk
- 1 can (12 ounces) whole-kernel corn, undrained
- 1 1/2 cups diced cooked ham
- Minced parsley

Melt butter in 3 1/2-quart saucepan. Sauté onion and green pepper until tender. Add potatoes, 2 cups water, salt, paprika, and pepper. Cover and simmer about 15 minutes, or until potatoes are tender. Combine flour and 1/3 cup water in small bowl; blend well. Stir into potato mixture. Add milk. Simmer until slightly thickened, stirring frequently. Add corn and ham; heat through. Sprinkle each serving with parsley.

Cauliflower-Potato Soup — 6 servings

- 3 cups chicken broth
- 1 head (2 pounds) cauliflower, thinly sliced (4 cups)
- 4 medium leeks (white part only) or 1 large onion, chopped
- 1 large potato, washed, peeled, and diced
- 1 cup half-and-half
- 1/4 teaspoon nutmeg
- 1/4 teaspoon salt
- 1/8 teaspoon white pepper
- Butter or margarine
- Nutmeg

Combine broth, cauliflower, leeks, and potato in 3-quart saucepan. Bring to a boil; cover and simmer 15 to 20 minutes, or until vegetables are tender. Place vegetables, 2 cups at a time, in bowl of food processor or blender container; purée. Return to saucepan. Add half-and-half, 1/4 teaspoon nutmeg, salt, and pepper. Heat through; do not boil. Dot each serving with butter and sprinkle with nutmeg.

Potato Chowder — 6 servings

- 2 slices bacon, cut into 1/2-inch pieces
- 1 medium onion, chopped
- 2 1/2 cups washed, diced, potatoes cut into 1/2-inch pieces
- 3/4 cup thinly sliced carrots
- 2 cups boiling water
- 1 teaspoon salt
- 3/4 teaspoon parsley flakes
- 1/4 teaspoon sage
- 1/4 teaspoon paprika
- 1/8 teaspoon white pepper
- 3 cups milk, divided
- 3 tablespoons all-purpose flour

Fry bacon in 3 1/2-quart saucepan until crisp. Remove bacon with slotted spoon; drain on paper towels. Crumble bacon; set aside. Add onion to drippings in saucepan; sauté until transparent. Add potatoes, carrots, water, and salt. Cover and simmer 10 minutes, or until vegetables are tender. Add parsley, sage, paprika, and pepper. Combine 1/2 cup milk and flour in 1-cup measure; blend thoroughly. Add to soup; simmer until slightly thickened, stirring constantly. Add remaining 2 1/2 cups milk; heat through. Sprinkle bacon on each serving.

Pumpkin-Potato Soup —————— 6 servings

- 2 tablespoons butter or margarine
- 1/4 cup minced onion
- 1 teaspoon curry powder
- 1 cup Mashed Potatoes (page 13)
- 3 cups chicken broth
- 1 can (16 ounces) pumpkin
- 1 teaspoon brown sugar
- 1/2 teaspoon salt
- 1/8 teaspoon pepper
- 1/8 teaspoon mace
- 1 cup half-and-half or milk
- Minced parsley or chives

Melt butter in 3-quart saucepan. Sauté onion until transparent. Remove from heat. Stir in curry powder, potatoes, broth, pumpkin, sugar, salt, pepper, and mace. Return to heat and cook, stirring often, until mixture begins to simmer. Stir in half-and-half. Heat through; do not boil. Sprinkle parsley or chives on each serving.

Potato Minestrone Soup ——— 10 to 12 servings

- 1 meaty beef soup bone
- 3 tablespoons salt
- 1 cup dried red kidney beans
- 1 pound beef for stew, cut into bite-size pieces
- 3 tablespoons olive oil
- 2 cloves garlic, minced
- 1/2 cup minced parsley
- 1 medium onion, chopped
- 1/4 teaspoon pepper
- 3 1/2 cups cut up fresh or canned tomatoes
- 2 cups finely shredded cabbage
- 1 1/2 cups cut green beans, cut into 1-inch pieces
- 1 cup diced celery
- 1 cup sliced carrots
- 2 cups washed, diced, potatoes
- 2 cups chopped fresh spinach
- 1/2 cup elbow macaroni
- Grated Parmesan cheese

Place soup bone, salt, beans, and 5 quarts water in 10-quart stockpot. Bring to a boil; skim foam. Cover and simmer 1 1/2 hours. Add stew meat; simmer 2 hours. Heat olive oil in small skillet. Add garlic, parsley, and onion; sauté until onion is transparent. Remove soup bone from soup; let cool until easily handled. Remove meat from bone; return meat to soup. Add onion mixture, pepper, tomatoes, cabbage, beans, celery, carrots, and potatoes. Bring to a boil; simmer 15 minutes. Add spinach and macaroni; simmer 20 minutes, or until macaroni is tender. Serve hot, topped with generous amounts of grated Parmesan cheese.

Fish-Potato Chowder — 6 servings

- 2 tablespoons butter or margarine
- 1 cup chopped onions
- 2 medium potatoes, washed and diced (2 cups)
- 1/2 cup thinly sliced celery
- 1/4 cup dry white wine
- 1 teaspoon salt
- 1/2 teaspoon dillweed
- 1/8 teaspoon pepper
- 1 small bay leaf
- 1 can (13 ounces) evaporated milk, undiluted
- 1 package (10 ounces) frozen haddock, cod, turbot, or similar fish, thawed and cut into 1 1/2 inch pieces

Melt butter in 3-quart saucepan. Sauté onions until transparent. Add potatoes, 2 cups water, celery, wine, salt, dillweed, pepper, and bay leaf. Cover and simmer 30 minutes, or until potatoes are tender. Stir in milk. Add fish. Heat to simmering; do not boil. Simmer until fish is opaque and flakes easily. Discard bay leaf.

Potato-Tomato Bisque — 6 to 8 servings

- 1/2 cup butter or margarine
- 1 medium onion, thinly sliced
- 4 cups peeled, chopped ripe tomatoes
- 1 cup tomato juice
- 3 medium potatoes, washed, peeled, and sliced (3 cups)
- 1/2 teaspoon salt
- 1/2 teaspoon tarragon
- 1/4 teaspoon rosemary
- 1/8 teaspoon white pepper
- 2 cups half-and-half, heated
- Minced parsley or chives

Melt butter in 3-quart saucepan. Sauté onion until transparent; do not brown. Add tomatoes and tomato juice; simmer until tomatoes are soft. Add potatoes, salt, tarragon, rosemary, and pepper. Simmer about 30 minutes, or until potatoes are tender, stirring occasionally. Remove from heat; cool slightly. Place mixture, 2 cups at a time, in bowl of food processor or blender container; purée. Return purée to saucepan; stir in half-and-half. Sprinkle parsley or chives on each serving.

Fish-Potato Chowder, Potato-Tomato Bisque

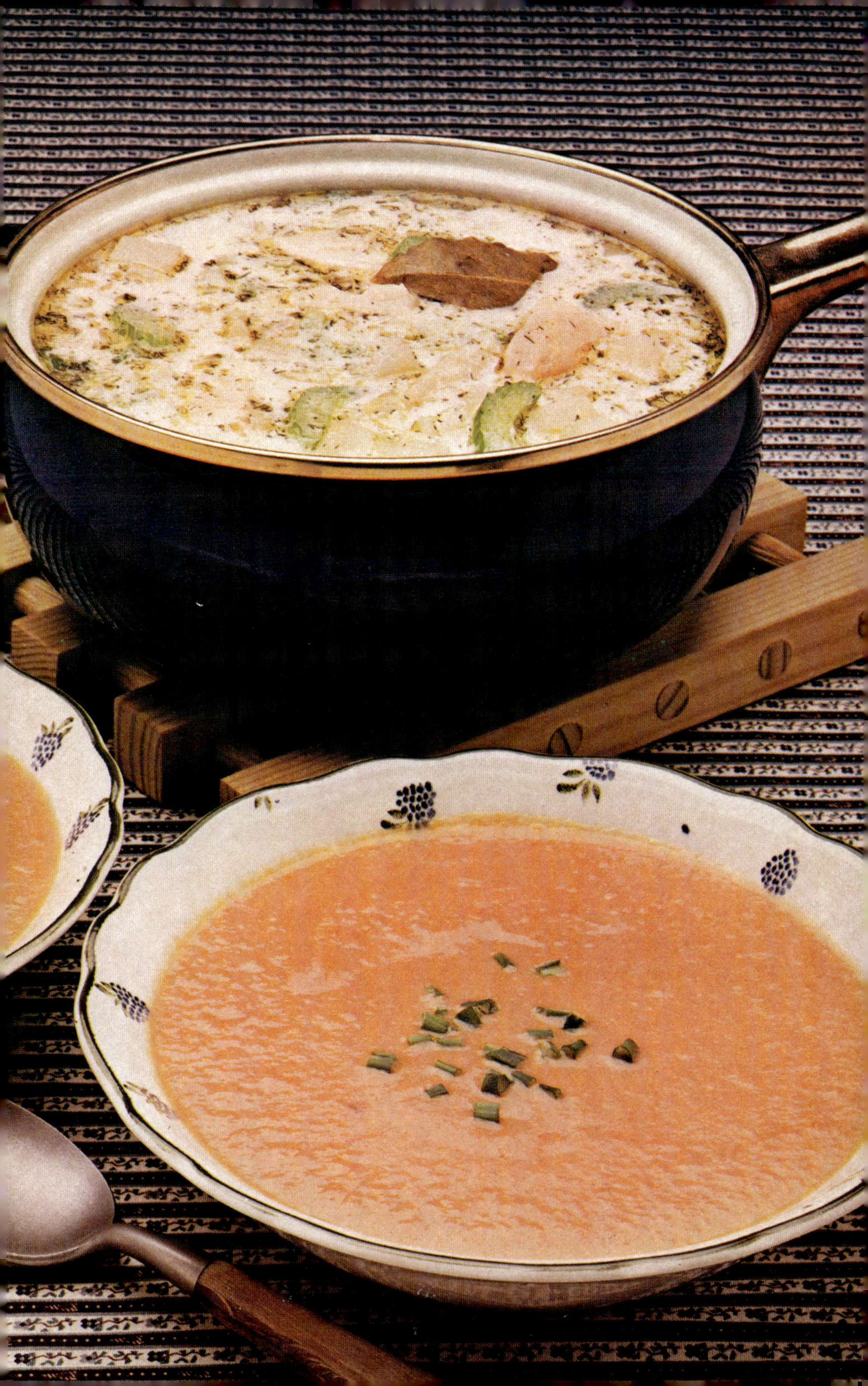

Vegetable Split Pea Soup ———— 8 servings

- 1 package (1 pound) split peas
- 1 can (28 ounces) tomatoes, undrained
- 1 cup chopped onions
- 1 meaty ham bone
- 1 large potato, washed, peeled and diced
- 3 carrots, peeled and diced
- 1 cup sliced celery
- 1/4 cup minced parsley
- 1/2 teaspoon salt
- 1 bay leaf
- Dash pepper
- Croutons

Combine split peas, tomatoes and liquid, onions, ham bone, and 2 quarts water in 6-quart stockpot or Dutch oven. Bring to a boil; cover and simmer 2 hours. Remove ham bone; let cool until easily handled. Remove meat from bone; return meat to soup. Add potato, carrots, celery, parsley, salt, bay leaf, and pepper. Simmer 30 minutes, or until vegetables are tender. Discard bay leaf. Serve hot topped with croutons.

Cream of Potato Soup ———— 6 servings

- 4 medium potatoes, washed, peeled, and cubed (3 cups)
- 4 medium onions, sliced
- 2 tablespoons butter or margarine
- 2 tablespoons all-purpose flour
- 3 cups milk, heated
- 2 teaspoons instant chicken bouillon granules
- 1 teaspoon salt
- 1/4 teaspoon white pepper
- Minced parsley

Combine potatoes, onions, and water to cover (about 4 cups) in 3 1/2-quart saucepan. Bring to a boil; cover and boil 20 minutes, or until potatoes are tender; drain, reserving 1 cup potato water. Process potatoes and onions through food mill or ricer. Blend butter and flour in saucepan. Stir in warm milk, bouillon, salt, pepper, and reserved potato water. Simmer until slightly thickened, stirring often. Stir in vegetables; heat through. Sprinkle parsley on each serving.

Senate Bean and Potato Soup
8 to 10 servings

- 1 package (1 pound) Great Northern beans
- 1 meaty ham bone or smoked pork hock
- 1 cup Mashed Potatoes (page 13)
- 2 cloves garlic, minced
- 1/4 cup minced parsley

Place beans in large bowl; add water to cover; let stand overnight. Drain beans. Place in 6-quart stockpot. Add ham bone and 3 quarts water. Bring to a boil; cover and simmer 2 hours. Stir in potatoes and garlic. Simmer 1 hour, or until beans are tender. Remove ham bone from stockpot; let cool until easily handled. Remove meat from bone; dice and return to soup. Add parsley; heat through.

Potato-Tuna Chowder
8 servings

- 2 tablespoons butter or margarine
- 1/2 cup chopped onion
- 6 medium potatoes, washed, peeled, and diced
- 2 medium carrots, peeled and diced
- 1/2 cup diced celery
- 1 can (9 1/4 ounces) tuna, undrained
- 4 cups milk
- 2 teaspoons salt
- 1/4 teaspoon white pepper
- 1/4 cup minced parsley

Melt butter in 3 1/2-quart saucepan. Sauté onion until transparent. Add potatoes, carrots, celery, and 2 cups water; bring to a boil. Cover and simmer 25 to 30 minutes, or until vegetables are tender, stirring occasionally. Add tuna and milk; heat through. Stir in salt and pepper. Sprinkle parsley on each serving.

Autumn Soup — 8 servings

- 1 pound lean ground beef
- 1 cup chopped onions
- 2 cups washed, diced potatoes
- 1 1/2 cups thinly sliced carrots
- 1 cup diced celery
- 3 beef bouillon cubes
- 1 clove garlic, minced
- 1 teaspoon salad herbs
- 1 bay leaf
- 1 teaspoon salt
- 1/4 teaspoon pepper
- 6 tomatoes, peeled and chopped

Brown beef in large saucepan or Dutch oven, stirring to break up beef. Add onions; cook 5 minutes. Drain fat. Add 2 quarts water, potatoes, carrots, celery, bouillon, garlic, salad herbs, bay leaf, salt, and pepper. Bring to a boil; cover and simmer 30 minutes, or until vegetables are tender. Add tomatoes; cover and simmer 10 minutes. Remove bay leaf. Serve hot.

Skillet Supper Salad — 6 servings

- 5 slices bacon
- 1 medium onion, chopped
- 3/4 cup sliced celery
- 6 frankfurters, cut diagonally into 1/2-inch slices
- 1 1/2 tablespoons all-purpose flour
- 1/3 cup vinegar
- 1 teaspoon salt
- 1/4 teaspoon pepper
- 2 teaspoons sugar
- 1 tablespoon prepared mustard
- 4 cups cooked, peeled, and sliced potatoes
- 1/2 teaspoon celery seed

Fry bacon in large skillet until crisp. Remove bacon with slotted spoon; drain on paper towels. Crumble; set aside. Add onion and celery to drippings in skillet; sauté until onion is transparent. Remove with slotted spoon to small bowl; set aside. Add frankfurters to drippings in skillet; brown on all sides; remove with slotted spoon to small bowl. Stir flour, vinegar, salt, pepper, and 3/4 cup water into drippings in skillet. Cook on moderate heat, stirring constantly until thickened. Stir in sugar and mustard. Add potatoes, frankfurters, onion mixture, and celery seed; stir just to combine. Simmer 10 minutes. Sprinkle bacon on top before serving. Serve warm.

Salmon Potato Salad ———————— 6 servings

- 4 medium potatoes, washed, cooked, peeled, and diced (4 cups)
- 1 can (16 ounces) red salmon, drained and flaked
- 2 cups minced celery
- 1/2 cup chopped green onions
- 1 envelope unflavored gelatin
- 2 tablespoons lemon juice
- 1/4 cup boiling water
- 1 1/2 cups mayonnaise
- 1 teaspoon salt
- 1/4 teaspoon cayenne
- Cherry tomatoes (optional)
- Parsley sprigs (optional)
- Paprika

Lightly oil a 6-cup ring-mold or bowl; set aside. Combine potatoes, salmon, celery, and onions in large bowl. Combine gelatin and lemon juice in small bowl; let stand 5 minutes to soften gelatin. Add boiling water; stir to dissolve. Stir in mayonnaise, salt, and cayenne; blend well. Pour over potato mixture; toss to coat evenly. Spoon evenly into prepared ring mold. Chill at least 1 hour. Unmold onto serving plate. Fill center of ring with cherry tomatoes and garnish with parsley, if desired. Sprinkle lightly with paprika.

German Potato Salad ———————— 8 to 10 servings

- 1/2 pound sliced bacon, cut into 1/2-inch pieces
- 1/2 cup chopped onion
- 1/2 cup sugar
- 2 tablespoons all-purpose flour
- 1/2 cup vinegar
- 1 teaspoon salt
- 1/4 teaspoon pepper
- 8 medium potatoes, washed, cooked, peeled, and sliced (8 cups)
- Minced parsley

Fry bacon in large skillet until crisp. Remove bacon with slotted spoon; drain on paper towels. Pour off all but 2 tablespoons drippings from skillet. Add onion; sauté until transparent. Combine sugar and flour; stir into onions in small bowl. Combine vinegar, 1 cup water, salt, and pepper in separate small bowl; stir into onions; cook, stirring constantly, until thickened. Combine bacon and potatoes in large bowl. Pour hot dressing over potatoes; stir gently to coat. Sprinkle with parsley. Serve warm.

Niçoise Salad

4 to 6 servings

- 1/4 cup red wine vinegar
- 3/4 cup olive or vegetable oil
- 2 tablespoons chopped green onion
- 2 tablespoons minced parsley
- 1 teaspoon dry mustard
- 1 1/4 teaspoon salt, divided
- 1/8 teaspoon pepper
- 4 large potatoes, washed; do not peel
- Ice water
- 1 pound green beans, trimmed
- 1 head Boston lettuce
- 1 can (7 ounces) tuna, drained and flaked
- 3 large tomatoes, peeled and quartered
- 3 hard-cooked eggs, quartered
- 1 can (2 ounces) flat anchovy fillets, drained
- 1/2 cup pitted ripe olives, quartered
- 1 tablespoon capers

Combine vinegar, oil, green onion, parsley, mustard, 1/4 teaspoon salt, and pepper in pint jar. Cover, shake to blend, set aside. Bring water and 1 teaspoon salt to a boil in large saucepan. Add potatoes; cover and boil 20 minutes, or until tender; drain. Plunge into ice water; drain. Peel and slice potatoes. Place in large bowl. Shake dressing; pour enough dressing over sliced potatoes just to coat; mix gently. Cover and refrigerate at least 2 hours. Cut beans into 1 1/2-inch pieces. Cook beans in boiling, salted water to cover 7 to 10 minutes, or until crisp-tender; drain. Plunge into ice water; drain. Pour enough dressing over beans just to coat. Cover and refrigerate until chilled. To serve, mound potatoes in center of lettuce-lined platter. Arrange tuna on top of potatoes. Alternately arrange beans, tomato, and eggs around edge of platter. Arrange anchovy fillets on top of beans. Garnish with capers and olives. Drizzle remaining dressing over all.

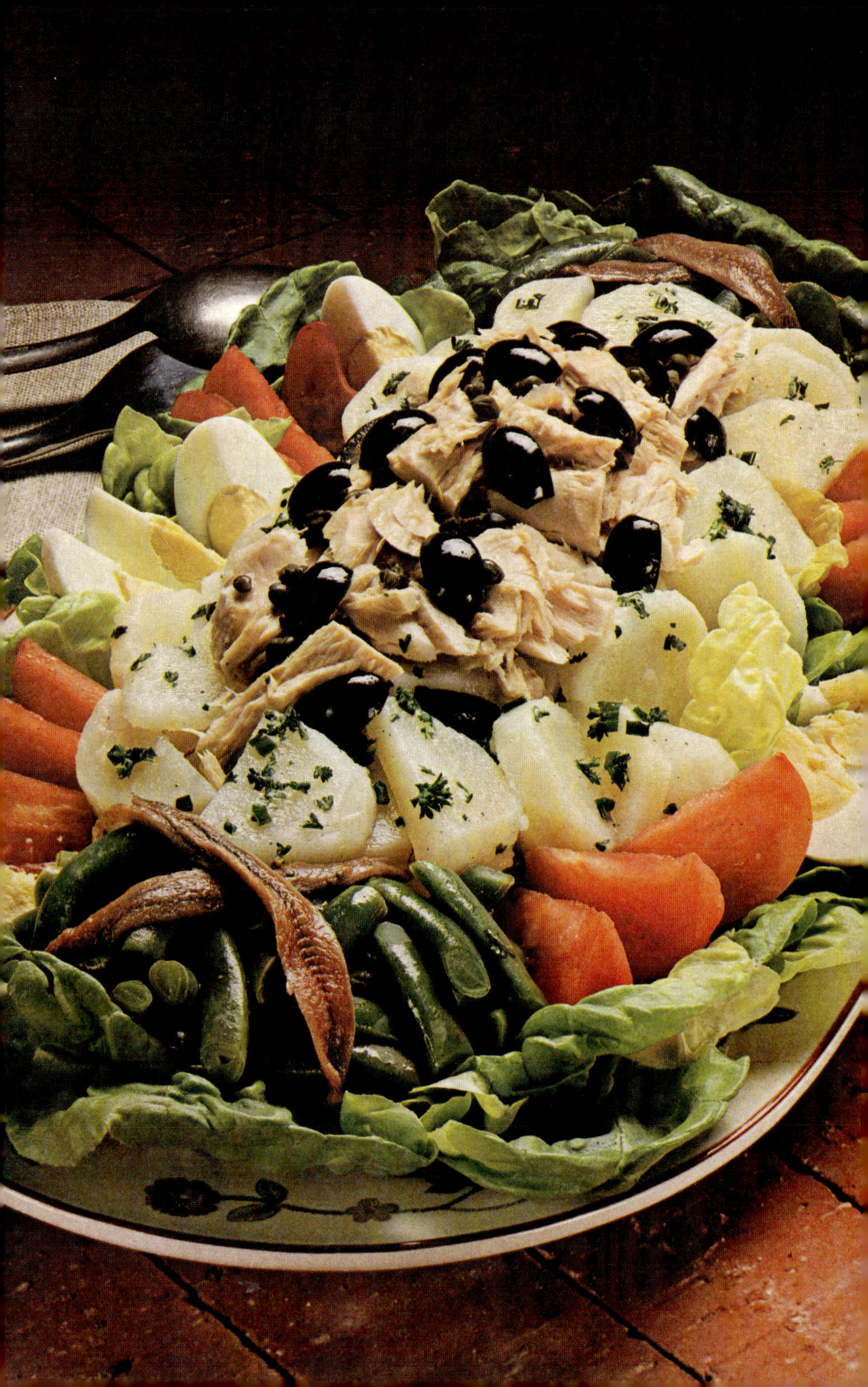

Knockwurst Potato Salad —— 6 to 8 servings

- 1 pound knockwurst or ring bologna, cooked, cooled, and cut diagonally into 1/2-inch slices
- 4 medium potatoes, washed, boiled, peeled, and sliced (4 cups)
- 1 red onion, thinly sliced, and separated into rings
- 1/2 cup sliced celery
- 3/4 cup Italian dressing
- 1/2 cup beer
- 2 teaspoons sugar
- 1/2 teaspoon caraway seed
- 2 quarts mixed salad greens

Combine knockwurst, potatoes, onion, and celery in large bowl; set aside. Combine salad dressing, beer, sugar, and caraway seed in small bowl. Pour over potato mixture; stir gently to coat. Cover and refrigerate at least 3 hours. Arrange salad greens in large salad bowl; spoon potato mixture over top; toss gently to coat.

Madison Avenue Potato Salad —— 6 servings

- 2 medium potatoes, washed, cooked, and diced (2 cups)
- 3 tablespoons vegetable oil
- 1 tablespoon wine vinegar
- 1 1/2 teaspoons salt
- 1/8 teaspoon pepper
- 1 cup thinly sliced celery
- 1/2 cup pitted and quartered ripe olives
- 2 hard-cooked eggs, sliced
- 1/4 cup diced dill pickle
- 1 jar (2 ounces) diced pimiento, drained
- 1 teaspoon minced onion
- 1 tablespoon prepared mustard
- 1/3 cup mayonnaise
- 1 head Boston lettuce

Place potatoes in refrigerator bowl. Blend oil, vinegar, salt, and pepper in separate bowl. Pour over potatoes; toss lightly. Cover and refrigerate until completely chilled. To serve, add celery, olives, eggs, pickle, and pimiento; toss lightly. Combine onion, mustard, and mayonnaise in small bowl; blend well. Pour over potato mixture; toss to mix. Serve in lettuce-lined bowl.

Calico Salad — 6 servings

- 1 package (10 ounces) frozen mixed vegetables, prepared according to package directions
- 1 large green pepper, seeded and diced
- 1 cup thinly sliced celery
- 1 large potato, washed, cooked, peeled, and cubed
- 1 small onion, chopped
- 1 can (15 ounces) red kidney beans, drained
- 1/4 cup minced parsley or 1 tablespoon parsley flakes
- 1/2 cup sugar
- 3 tablespoons all-purpose flour
- 5 teaspoons prepared mustard
- 1/2 cup cider vinegar

Combine mixed vegetables, green pepper, celery, potato, onion, kidney beans, and parsley in large bowl; cover and refrigerate. Combine sugar, flour, mustard, and vinegar in small saucepan. Cook on moderate heat, stirring constantly, until mixture thickens. Remove from heat; set aside to cool. Pour over vegetables. Do not mix. Cover and refrigerate at least 8 hours or overnight.

Potato Salad Romano — 6 servings

- 3 pounds small red potatoes, washed
- Ice water
- 1/2 pound Swiss cheese, cut into 2 × 1/8-inch strips
- 1 1/2 cups mayonnaise
- 1 teaspoon minced chives
- 3/4 teaspoon salt
- 1/4 teaspoon cayenne
- 1/4 pound diced cooked ham
- 2 large fresh mushrooms, sliced

Place potatoes in large saucepan; add water to cover. Bring to a boil; cover and simmer 20 minutes, or until tender; drain. Plunge into ice water; let stand until cool enough to handle; drain. Peel and thinly slice potatoes. Combine potatoes and cheese in large bowl. Combine mayonnaise, chives, salt, and cayenne in separate bowl; blend well. Spoon mayonnaise mixture over potatoes and cheese; stir gently to coat. Cover and refrigerate at least 5 to 6 hours, or overnight. Sprinkle with ham. Garnish with mushroom slices.

French Potato Salad ———————— 10 servings

- 1 pound sliced bacon
- 3 pounds small red potatoes, washed, unpeeled, cooked, and cut into 1/4-inch slices
- 1/2 cup olive or vegetable oil
- 1/2 cup sliced green onions
- 1/4 cup beef consommé
- 1/4 cup minced parsley
- 1 teaspoon salt
- 1 teaspoon dry mustard
- 1/2 teaspoon basil
- 1/2 teaspoon tarragon
- 1 clove garlic, minced
- Dash pepper

Fry bacon in large skillet until crisp. Remove bacon with slotted spoon; drain on paper towels, crumble. Combine bacon and potatoes in mixing bowl; set aside. Combine remaining ingredients in small saucepan. Bring to a boil on low heat. Pour over potato-bacon mixture; toss lightly to mix. Serve warm.

Superb Garden Salad ———————— 6 to 8 servings

- 1 cup whole green beans, trimmed
- 4 medium potatoes, washed, cooked, peeled, and diced (4 cups)
- 2 tomatoes, cut into wedges
- 10 radishes, sliced
- 1/2 cucumber, peeled and sliced
- 10 green onions, cut into 1/2-inch pieces
- 4 cups lettuce, romaine, and endive (mixed)
- 1 cup Italian dressing

Cook green beans in water until crisp-tender; drain. Plunge into ice water; let stand until cool; drain. Combine potatoes, beans, tomatoes, radishes, cucumber, green onions, and salad greens in large salad bowl. Drizzle on salad dressing; toss lightly to mix. Serve immediately.

Creamy Potato Salad ——————— 6 servings

- 6 medium potatoes, washed
- 1/2 cup mayonnaise
- 2 tablespoons light cream or half-and-half
- 2 tablespoons minced onion
- 2 teaspoons cider vinegar
- 1 1/4 teaspoons salt
- 1 teaspoon prepared mustard
- 1/8 teaspoon coarsely ground pepper
- 1/3 cup minced green pepper
- 1 cup thinly sliced celery
- 1/4 cup minced parsley
- Lettuce leaves

Place potatoes in large saucepan; add water to cover. Bring to a boil; cover and boil 25 to 30 minutes, or until tender; drain. Cool potatoes until easily handled. Peel and cut into bite-size pieces (6 cups). Combine mayonnaise, cream, onion, vinegar, salt, mustard, and pepper in large bowl; blend well. Stir in potatoes, green pepper, celery, and parsley; chill. Serve on lettuce leaves.

Three hard-cooked eggs can be added to potatoes or used for garnish, if desired.

Apple-Potato Salad ——————— 8 servings

- 6 medium potatoes, washed, cooked, and sliced (6 cups)
- 2 cups thinly sliced red apples
- 1 cup diced celery
- 1/2 cup diced green pepper
- 1/4 cup minced onion
- 1 cup dairy sour cream or plain yogurt
- 1/2 cup mayonnaise
- 1 teaspoon salt
- 1/4 teaspoon celery seed
- Dash pepper
- Mixed salad greens
- 1/4 cup coarsely chopped walnuts or pecans

Combine potatoes, apples, celery, green pepper, and onion in large bowl. Combine sour cream, mayonnaise, salt, celery seed, and pepper in small bowl; blend well. Stir into potato mixture; blend well. Cover and chill several hours to blend flavors. Arrange salad greens in large salad bowl or on individual plates. Spoon potato salad on top. Sprinkle with nuts.

Party Ham and Potato Salad

8 servings

- 9 slices boiled ham, divided
- 1 envelope unflavored gelatin
- 2 teaspoons cider vinegar
- 1/3 cup boiling water
- 3/4 cup mayonnaise
- 1 teaspoon prepared mustard
- 2 teaspoons minced onion
- 6 medium potatoes, washed, cooked, and diced (6 cups)
- 1/2 cup thinly sliced celery
- 1/4 cup minced green pepper
- 1 jar (2 ounces) diced pimiento, drained
- 3 hard-cooked eggs, sliced
- 1 head Boston lettuce
- Parsley sprigs

Line 9×5-inch loaf pan with 2 strips waxed paper — 1 lengthwise, 1 crosswise. Line pan with 3 ham slices, covering bottom and sides completely. Mince 5 ham slices; set aside. Combine gelatin and vinegar in small bowl; let stand 5 minutes to soften. Add boiling water; stir to dissolve gelatin. Combine mayonnaise, mustard, onion, and gelatin in large bowl; blend well. Stir in potatoes, celery, green pepper, minced ham, pimiento, and all but 5 egg slices; stir gently to blend. Pour into prepared loaf pan; press lightly to smooth top. Cover with remaining ham slice. Cover pan with plastic wrap; refrigerate 1 hour, or until set. To serve, turn out onto lettuce-lined platter; peel and discard waxed paper. Garnish with reserved egg slices and parsley sprigs. Slice to serve.

Dinner's On the Table

And now, the moment you've been waiting for, starring, what else, but the peerless potato. Choose from any of these main attractions for tonight's dinner. Lest you fear the same-old-thing treatment: Have you ever thought of using potatoes to stuff green peppers? Spudzagna? So bring out the family and bring on the potatoes. Applause will not be necessary, but will be greatly appreciated.

Red Flannel Hash — 6 servings

- 2 cups coarsely chopped cooked corned beef
- 5 large potatoes, washed, cooked, peeled, and coarsely chopped
- 6 medium beets, cooked, peeled, and chopped
- 1 medium onion, chopped
- 1/2 cup beef bouillon
- 1/2 teaspoon salt
- 1/8 teaspoon pepper

Preheat oven to 350°F. Grease a 2-quart casserole; set aside. Combine all ingredients in large bowl; blend thoroughly. Pack into prepared casserole. Bake, uncovered, 30 minutes, or until heated through and golden brown.

You can also prepare this dish by heating 3 tablespoons butter or margarine in large skillet. Combine all ingredients in skillet. Cook on moderate heat until brown on bottom. Fold in half. Remove to warm serving platter.

Country Stew
_____ 6 servings

- 5 pounds short ribs, trimmed and cut into 2-inch pieces
- 1/2 cup all-purpose flour
- 1/4 cup vegetable oil
- 2/3 cup dry red wine
- 1 medium onion, chopped
- 1 clove garlic, minced
- 2 teaspoons salt
- 1/4 teaspoon pepper
- 2 beef bouillon cubes
- 6 large potatoes, washed, peeled, and quartered
- 1/2 pound small fresh mushrooms, cleaned and trimmed
- 1 package (10 ounces) frozen whole green beans
- 1 can (16 ounces) peeled whole tomatoes, undrained

Dredge ribs in flour to coat; reserve leftover flour. Heat oil in 8-quart Dutch oven on moderate heat. Add ribs; brown on all sides. Remove ribs. Stir in reserved flour. While stirring, add 1 cup water and wine; stir until thickened. Return ribs to pan. Add onion, garlic, salt, pepper, and bouillon. Bring to a boil; cover and simmer about 1 hour, or until tender. Remove ribs with slotted spoon; keep warm. Add potatoes, mushrooms, and beans. Simmer 20 to 30 minutes, or until vegetables are tender. Add ribs and tomatoes with liquid; heat through. Use slotted spoon to remove meat and vegetables to large serving platter. Pass gravy with ribs.

One-Dish Deluxe
_____ 4 to 6 servings

- 1 pound lean ground beef
- 2 eggs, slightly beaten
- 1 medium onion, chopped
- 12 soda crackers, crushed
- 1 teaspoon salt
- 1/4 teaspoon pepper
- 3 large potatoes, washed, peeled, and halved lengthwise
- 5 slices bacon

Preheat oven to 350°F. Grease a 3 1/2-quart casserole; set aside. Combine beef, eggs, onion, cracker crumbs, salt, and pepper in large bowl; blend thoroughly. Shape into round loaf. Place in prepared casserole. Arrange potatoes around edge of meatloaf. Arrange bacon over meatloaf and potatoes. Bake 60 minutes, or until meatloaf is done and potatoes are tender. Slice meatloaf. Arrange on serving platter along with potatoes.

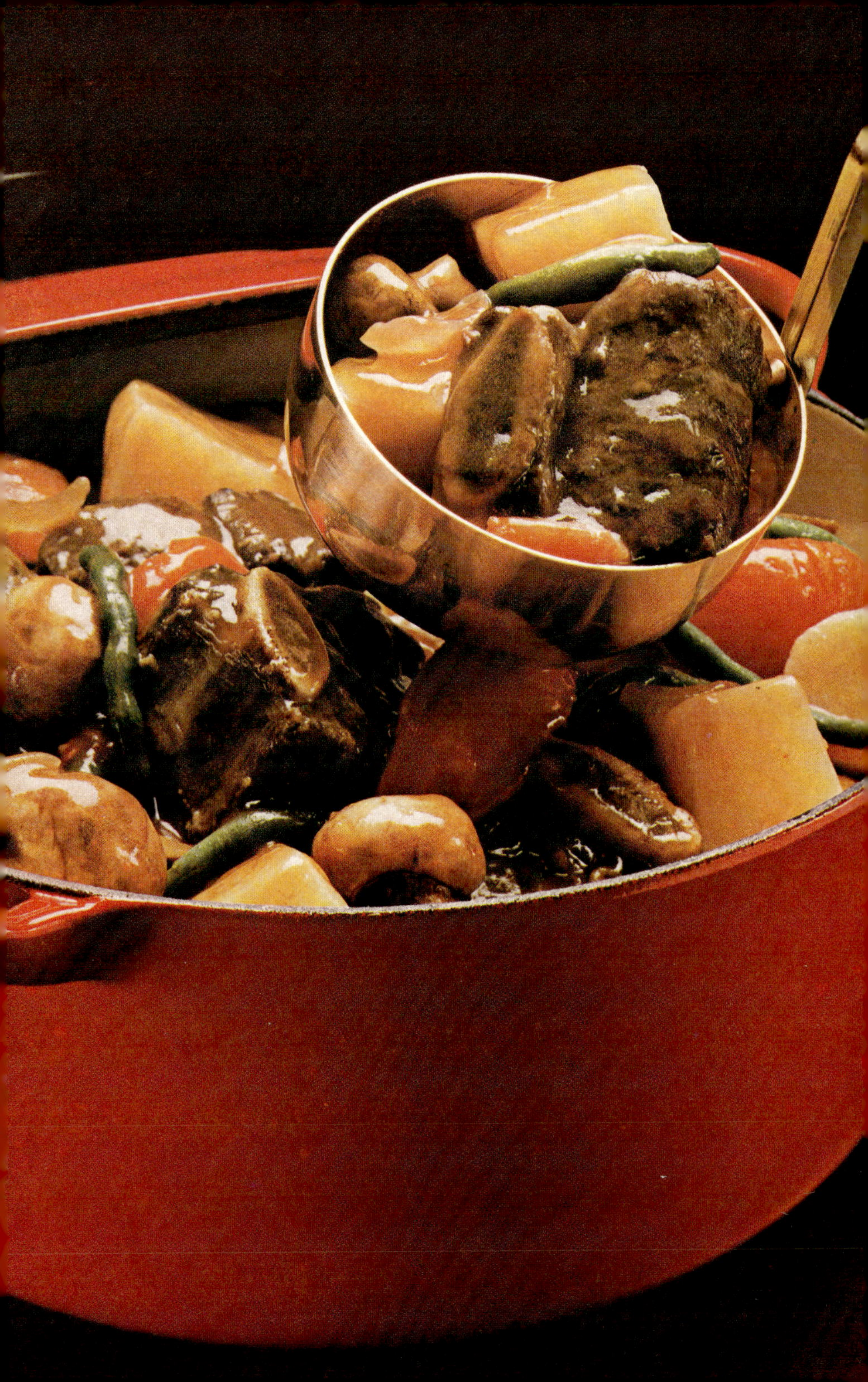

Spudzagna
_____ 8 to 10 servings

- 1 1/2 pounds bulk Italian sausage, crumbled
- 1 medium onion, chopped
- 2 teaspoons seasoned salt
- 1/2 teaspoon pepper
- 1 can (14 1/2 ounces) stewed tomatoes, drained
- 1 can (10 3/4 ounces) tomato purée
- 1 teaspoon garlic powder
- 1/2 teaspoon hot pepper sauce
- 1 cup shredded mozzarella cheese
- 1 cup shredded Cheddar cheese
- 5 medium potatoes, washed peeled, and thinly sliced
- 1 1/2 cups ricotta cheese
- 1/2 cup grated Parmesan or Romano cheese

Combine sausage, onion, salt, and pepper in large skillet; cook on moderate heat 10 minutes, or until sausage is no longer pink. Drain; set aside. Combine tomatoes, tomato purée, garlic powder, and hot pepper sauce in small bowl; set aside. Combine mozzarella and Cheddar cheese in another small bowl; mix lightly. Preheat oven to 350°F. Arrange one-third of potatoes over bottom of 9 × 13-inch baking dish. Spread meat mixture evenly over potatoes. Spoon on half of the tomato mixture. Sprinkle with one-third of the cheese mixture. Arrange one-third of the potatoes on top; pack down firmly. Spoon on remaining tomato mixture. Spread ricotta cheese on top. Sprinkle with one-third of the cheese mixture. Cover evenly with remaining potatoes. Sprinkle with remaining cheese mixture. Sprinkle with Parmesan cheese. Pack down firmly. Bake 60 minutes, or until potatoes are tender and top is golden brown.

Lunch Patties
_____ 4 to 5 servings

- 2/3 cup shredded raw potato
- 1 pound lean ground beef
- 1 egg, slightly beaten
- 1/4 cup minced onion
- 1 teaspoon salt
- 1/4 teaspoon pepper
- 1 tablespoon vegetable oil
- 1 cup tomato juice
- 1 tablespoon all-purpose flour

Combine potato, beef, egg, onion, salt, and pepper in large bowl; blend well. Shape into 4 or 5 patties. Heat oil in large skillet on medium high heat. Brown patties on both sides. Add tomato juice. Cover and simmer 15 minutes, or until patties are cooked. Use spatula to remove patties to warm platter; keep warm. Combine flour and 1/3 cup water in 1-cup measure; blend thoroughly. Stir into pan juices. Cook until thickened, stirring often. Serve over patties.

Hearty Beef Stew _____ 4 servings

- 1 1/2 pounds beef for stew, cut into bite-size pieces
- 1 can (16 ounces) stewed tomatoes, undrained
- 2 large potatoes, washed, peeled, and diced
- 2 carrots, peeled and cut into 1/2-inch slices
- 1 cup frozen small onions
- 1/2 cup fresh or frozen peas
- 3 tablespoons quick-cooking tapioca
- 1 tablespoon sugar
- 1 teaspoon salt
- 1/4 teaspoon pepper

Preheat oven to 250°F. Combine beef, tomatoes and liquid, potatoes, carrots, onions, and peas in 3-quart casserole. Combine tapioca, sugar, salt, and pepper in small dish; mix lightly. Pour over ingredients in casserole; stir just to blend. Cover and bake 4 hours. Remove from oven; stir lightly. Serve hot.

Mushroom-Beef and Duchess Potatoes _____ 4 to 6 servings

- Duchess Potatoes (page 75)
- 2 tablespoons grated Parmesan cheese
- 1/4 cup butter or margarine
- 1/2 pound fresh mushrooms, quartered
- 1 pound lean ground beef
- 1/3 cup dry red wine
- 1/2 cup chopped green onions
- 1 tablespoon all-purpose flour
- 3/4 cup heavy cream
- 1/4 cup minced parsley

Preheat oven to 400°F. Spoon Duchess Potatoes in a border around edge of 10-inch round heatproof platter. Sprinkle cheese evenly over potatoes. Bake 15 minutes, or until golden brown. While potatoes are browning, melt butter in large skillet on moderate heat. Add mushrooms; sauté until almost tender. Push mushrooms to one side of skillet. Add beef. Cook until browned, stirring constantly; drain fat. Stir wine into mushrooms and beef; bring to a boil. Add onion. Combine flour and cream in small bowl; blend thoroughly. Stir into beef mixture. Cook until thickened, stirring constantly. Spoon mixture inside potato border. Sprinkle with parsley before serving.

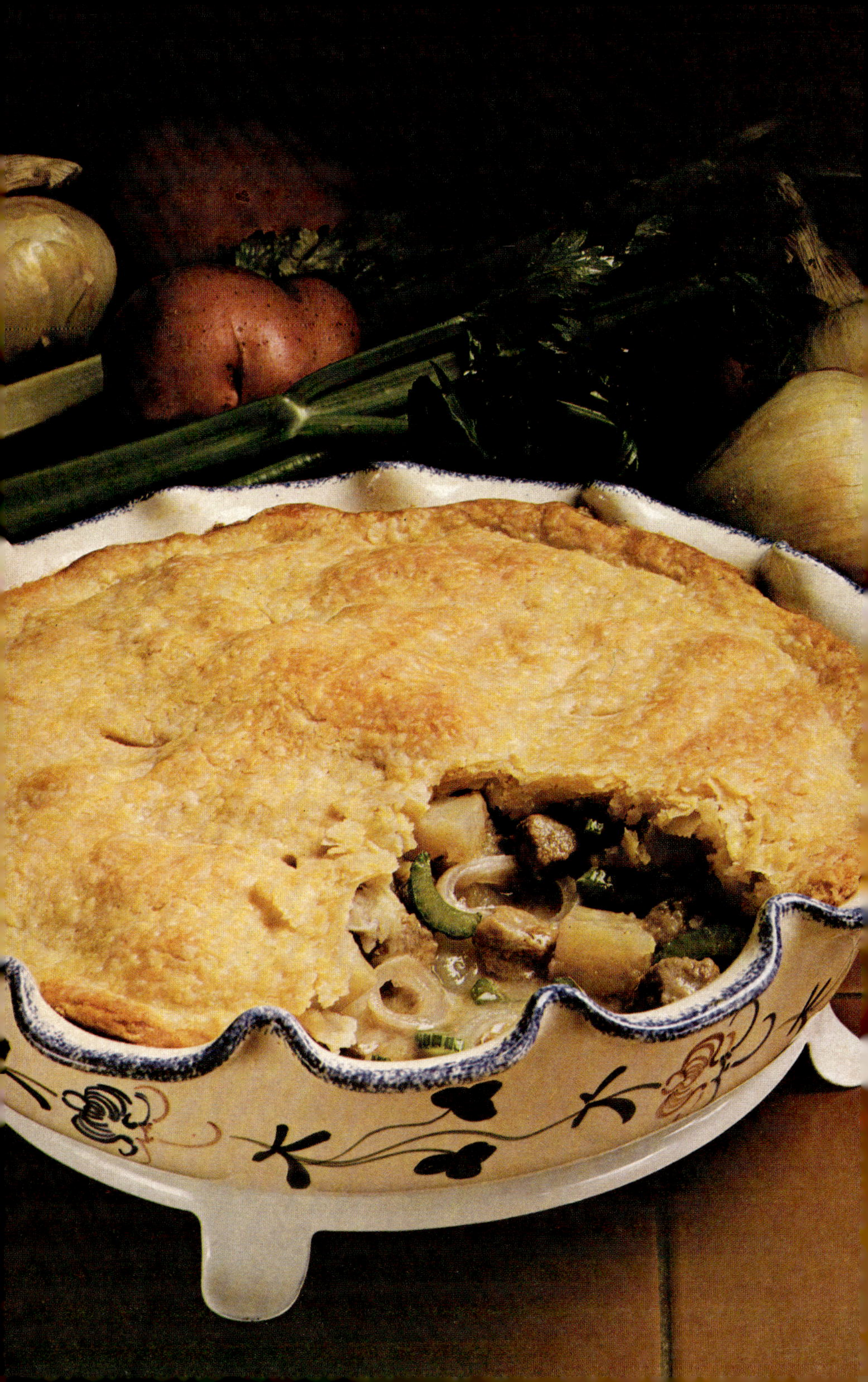

Onion, Steak, and Potato Pie

6 servings

- 1/4 cup vegetable shortening
- 1 cup sliced onions
- 1/4 cup sliced celery
- 1/4 cup all-purpose flour
- 1 teaspoon salt
- 1/8 teaspoon pepper
- 1 pound round steak, cut into 1-inch cubes
- 2 1/2 cups boiling water
- 2 medium potatoes, washed, cooked, peeled, and diced
- 1 Potato Crust (page 141), unbaked

Heat shortening in heavy 3-quart saucepan. Sauté onions and celery until onions are transparent. Use slotted spoon to remove onions and celery to small bowl; set aside. Combine flour, salt, and pepper in shallow dish; dredge steak in flour to coat all sides. Brown in saucepan used to sauté onions. Pour boiling water over steak. Cover and simmer 45 minutes, or until tender. Add potatoes and onion-celery mixture. Cook on low heat 10 minutes. Preheat oven to 450°F. Pour mixture into 9-inch deep-dish pie plate. Fit crust over top; trim and flute edges; cut several slits in crust. Bake 20 to 25 minutes, or until golden brown.

Hamburger Casserole

4 servings

- 1 pound lean ground beef
- 1 cup chopped onions
- 1 medium potato, washed, peeled, and shredded (1 cup)
- 1 cup peeled and diced carrots
- 1 cup sliced celery
- 1 teaspoon Worcestershire sauce
- 1/2 teaspoon salt
- 1/4 teaspoon pepper
- 1 can (10 3/4 ounces) cream of tomato soup, undiluted
- 1/2 cup crushed Potato Chips (page 18)

Preheat oven to 350°F. Place beef and onion in heavy skillet; cook until beef is no longer red and onion is transparent, stirring to break up beef; drain fat. Combine beef-onion mixture, potatoes, carrots, celery, Worcestershire, salt, and pepper in 2-quart casserole. Spoon soup over top. Sprinkle crushed chips evenly over top. Bake, uncovered, 40 minutes, or until vegetables are tender.

Onion, Steak, and Potato Pie

Kraut and Potato Casserole —— 10 servings

- 5 cups sliced potatoes
- 1 1/2 pounds lean ground beef
- 1 small onion, chopped
- 1/2 teaspoon salt
- 1 can (16 ounces) sauerkraut, drained
- 1 can (10 1/2 ounces) cream of chicken soup, undiluted
- 1 can (10 3/4 ounces) cream of mushroom soup, undiluted

Butter a 9 × 13-inch baking dish. Arrange potatoes in prepared dish. Place beef and onion in large skillet; cook until beef is no longer red and onion is transparent, stirring to break up beef. Drain fat. Preheat oven to 350°F. Spoon beef and onion over potatoes; sprinkle with salt. Arrange sauerkraut on top. Combine soups and 1/2 cup water in small bowl; blend well. Spread over casserole. Bake, uncovered, 1 to 1 1/2 hours, or until potatoes are tender.

Potatoes can be peeled or unpeeled without affecting the appearance of the casserole.

Potatoes and Meatball Casserole —— 4 servings

- 3/4 pound lean ground beef
- 1/4 cup minced onion
- 1 teaspoon Worcestershire sauce
- 1/2 teaspoon salt
- 1/2 teaspoon parsley flakes
- Dash pepper
- 1 tablespoon vegetable oil
- 1 pound small red potatoes, washed, cooked, and peeled
- 1 can (10 3/4 ounces) cream of mushroom soup, undiluted
- 1/2 cup crushed Potato Chips (page 18)

Preheat oven to 350°F. Combine beef, onion, Worcestershire, salt, parsley, and pepper in medium bowl; blend well. Shape into 1-inch balls. Heat oil in skillet. Carefully brown meatballs on all sides; drain. Arrange meatballs and potatoes in 1 3/4-quart casserole. Combine soup and 1/2 cup water in small bowl; blend well. Pour over ingredients in casserole. Sprinkle crushed chips evenly over top. Bake, uncovered 20 minutes, or until heated through.

Roast Pork with Potatoes ——— 8 servings

- 2 cloves garlic
- 1 boneless pork roast (5 pounds)
- 1 teaspoon salt
- 1 teaspoon thyme
- 1 bay leaf, crumbled
- 1/4 teaspoon white pepper
- 1 medium onion, chopped
- 1/2 cup carrots
- 2 sprigs parsley
- 2 tablespoons all-purpose flour
- 1 can (10 3/4 ounces) chicken broth
- 4 large potatoes, washed, peeled and quartered, or 2 pounds small potatoes, washed and peeled
- 1/4 cup butter or margarine, melted
- Minced parsley

Preheat oven to 425°F. Cut 1 clove garlic in half. Rub outside of pork with cut sides of garlic. Sliver remaining garlic clove. Make 6 shallow slits in top of roast. Insert a garlic sliver into each slit. Combine salt, thyme, bay leaf, and pepper in small dish. Rub mixture over entire surface of roast. Place onion, carrots, and parsley in center of shallow roasting pan. Insert meat thermometer in center of roast. Place roast, fat-side up, on top of vegetables. Roast, uncovered, 1 hour. Remove roast from pan, set aside. Pour off all but 1 tablespoon drippings. Place pan on stove top on low heat. Stir flour into drippings in pan; cook and stir to brown flour. Gradually stir in chicken broth. Stir in 3/4 cup water. Bring to a boil; simmer until gravy is thickened, stirring constantly and scraping browned bits from bottom of pan. Strain gravy through sieve; discard vegetables. Pour gravy into saucepan; set aside. Return roast to roasting pan. Arrange potatoes around roast. Brush with half of the melted butter. Reduce oven to 400°F. Roast about 1 hour, or until 170°F on thermometer and potatoes are tender. After 20 minutes roasting time, turn potatoes; brush on remaining butter. To serve, sprinkle with parsley. Reheat gravy in saucepan. Pass gravy with roast and potatoes.

Ham and Potatoes au Gratin — 4 servings

- 1/3 cup butter or margarine, divided
- 3 tablespoons all-purpose flour
- 1 1/2 cups milk, heated
- 1 cup shredded sharp Cheddar cheese
- 1 cup diced cooked ham
- 1 tablespoon onion flakes
- 2 cups sliced cooked potatoes, divided
- 1 tablespoon minced parsley

Preheat oven to 400°F. Butter a 2-quart casserole; set aside. Melt 3 tablespoons butter in a 2-quart saucepan on moderate heat. Add flour; cook 2 minutes, stirring constantly. Add milk; cook until thickened, stirring constantly. Add cheese; stir until melted. Remove from heat. Stir in ham, onion flakes, and 1 cup potatoes. Pour into prepared casserole. Arrange remaining potatoes on top. Melt remaining butter; brush on potatoes. Sprinkle with parsley. Bake 20 minutes, or until heated through.

Potato Paprika with Smoked Sausage — 6 servings

- 1 can (8 ounces) tomato sauce
- 1/2 cup beef bouillon
- 1 tablespoon vinegar
- 1 teaspoon paprika
- 1/4 teaspoon caraway seed
- 1 tablespoon butter or margarine
- 1 medium onion, chopped
- 1 pound smoked sausage (Kielbasa), casing removed, cut into 1 1/2-inch pieces
- 2 pounds potatoes, washed, peeled, and cut into 1 1/2-inch pieces
- 2 tablespoons minced parsley

Combine tomato sauce, bouillon, vinegar, paprika, and caraway seed in small bowl; set aside. Heat butter in large skillet. Sauté onion until golden brown. Add sausage and potatoes. Stir in tomato sauce mixture. Bring to a boil; cover and simmer 30 minutes, or until potatoes are tender. Sprinkle with parsley before serving.

Bacon and Potato Puff ───────── 6 servings

- 1/2 pound sliced bacon
- 4 eggs, separated
- 2 cups Mashed Potatoes (page 13), hot
- 2 tablespoons butter or margarine
- 1/4 cup grated onion
- 1/2 teaspoon dry mustard
- 1/8 teaspoon white pepper
- 3 drops hot pepper sauce
- 1/2 cup shredded sharp Cheddar cheese
- 1/2 cup minced parsley

Fry bacon in skillet until crisp. Remove bacon with slotted spoon; drain on paper towels; crumble. Preheat oven to 325°F. Beat egg whites in small bowl until stiff but not dry; set aside. Combine potatoes, butter, egg yolks, onion, mustard, pepper, and hot pepper sauce in large bowl; blend thoroughly. Add bacon, cheese, and parsley. Carefully fold egg whites into potato mixture until just blended. Turn into 1 1/2-quart straight-sided casserole or soufflé dish. Bake 50 to 52 minutes, or until golden brown. Serve immediately.

Potato, Cheese and Bacon Casserole ───────── 12 servings

- 1/2 pound sliced bacon, cut in 1-inch pieces
- 8 medium potatoes, washed, cooked, peeled and diced
- 1 pound process American cheese, sliced and cut into strips
- 1 cup mayonnaise
- 1/2 cup chopped onion
- 1/2 teaspoon salt
- 1/8 teaspoon pepper
- 1/4 cup sliced stuffed olives

Preheat oven to 350°F. Butter a 9 × 13-inch baking dish; set aside. Fry bacon in skillet until limp; remove bacon with slotted spoon; drain; set aside. Combine potatoes, cheese, mayonnaise, onion, salt, and pepper. Spoon into prepared baking dish. Sprinkle with bacon and olives. Bake, uncovered, 1 hour, or until heated through.

This recipe can easily be cut in half.

Potato Stuffed Peppers ———————— 6 servings

- 6 large green peppers
- 6 tablespoons butter or margarine
- 4 medium potatoes, washed, cooked, peeled, and cut into 1/2-inch cubes
- 1 medium onion, chopped
- 2 teaspoons lemon juice
- 1 teaspoon salt
- 1/2 teaspoon coriander
- 1/2 teaspoon cumin
- 1/2 teaspoon dry mustard
- 1/2 teaspoon turmeric or curry powder
- 1/8 teaspoon pepper

Cut a slice from top of each pepper; carefully remove seeds, keeping shells intact. Remove stem portion from tops; discard. Chop remaining part of tops; set aside. Bring 4 quarts salted water to a boil. Drop shells into water. Boil 3 minutes; remove from water; rinse in cold water. Turn upside down on paper towels to drain. Preheat oven to 350°F. Melt butter on moderate heat in large skillet. Add potatoes, onion, and reserved chopped pepper. Cook on moderate heat until potatoes are lightly browned. Remove from heat. Stir in lemon juice and seasonings. Arrange pepper shells, cut-side up, in shallow baking dish. Spoon potato mixture into shells. Bake, uncovered, 20 minutes, or until heated through.

Frankfurter Wonder ———————— 6 servings

- 3 medium potatoes, washed, peeled, and sliced
- 1 medium onion, chopped
- 1 small green pepper, seeded and chopped
- 1/2 teaspoon salt
- 1/4 teaspoon pepper
- 1/4 teaspoon celery seed
- 5 frankfurters (1/2 pound), cut into 1-inch pieces
- 1 can (10 3/4 ounces) cream of celery soup, undiluted

Preheat oven to 350°F. Butter a 2-quart casserole. Arrange half of the potatoes in prepared casserole. Layer half of the onion and green pepper over potatoes. Sprinkle with salt, pepper, and celery seed. Place all of the frankfurters in casserole. Repeat layers with remaining vegetables. Combine soup and 1/4 cup water in small bowl; blend well. Pour over ingredients in casserole. Cover and bake 60 to 70 minutes, or until vegetables are tender. Stir before serving.

Potato Stuffed Peppers

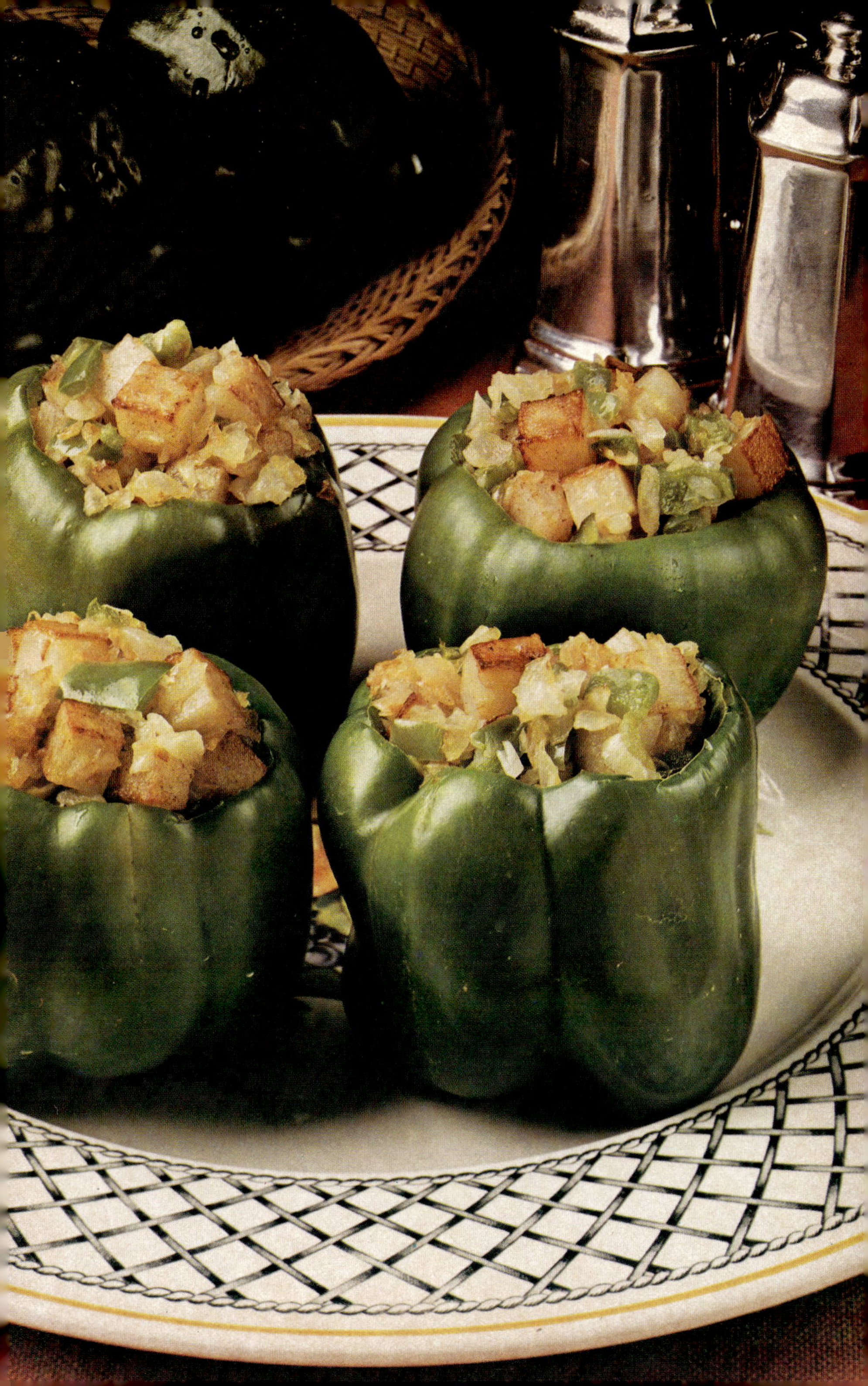

Lamb and Lima Stew ———————— 8 servings

- 1 cup dried white lima beans
- 1 tablespoon vegetable oil
- 2 pounds lamb, cut into bite-size pieces
- 1/2 teaspoon salt
- 1/4 teaspoon pepper
- 1/4 teaspoon thyme
- 2 large onions, quartered
- 3 medium potatoes, washed peeled, and cut into eighths
- 4 large carrots, peeled and cut into 1 1/2-inch pieces
- 3 tablespoons all-purpose flour
- 1/3 cup cold water
- 1/4 cup minced parsley

Bring 1 quart water to a boil in medium saucepan. Add beans; bring to a brisk boil; boil 2 minutes. Remove from heat; let stand 1 hour. (Beans can also be soaked overnight in water.) Heat oil in 5-quart Dutch oven. Add lamb; brown on all sides. Add beans and water, salt, pepper, and thyme. Cover and simmer 1 1/2 hours, or until beans and meat are tender. Preheat oven to 350°F. Add onions, potatoes, and carrots to meat mixture. Combine flour and cold water in small bowl; blend thoroughly. Stir into meat mixture. Stir so that vegetables are in lower portion of pan and completely covered with liquid. Add more water, if necessary. Bake, uncovered, 50 to 60 minutes, or until vegetables are tender. Spoon into warm serving dish. Sprinkle with parsley.

Chicken Fricassee ———————— 6 servings

- 1 broiler-fryer (3 1/2 to 4 pounds), cut up
- 1 medium onion, sliced
- 2 stalks celery, sliced
- 2 cloves garlic, crushed
- 1 tablespoon salt
- 1/2 teaspoon pepper
- 5 medium potatoes, washed, peeled, and halved
- 4 carrots, peeled and thinly sliced
- 1 package (10 ounces) frozen peas
- 1/2 cup all-purpose flour
- 1/2 cup water
- Potato Dumplings (page 82)

Combine chicken, onion, celery, garlic, salt, pepper, and 6 cups water in large saucepan. Bring to a boil; simmer 30 to 40 minutes, or until chicken is tender. Remove chicken from saucepan; let cool until easily handled. Remove skin and meat from bones; cut meat into chunks. Return to broth. Add potatoes, carrots, and peas. Cook on medium low heat 30 minutes, or until vegetables are tender. Remove 2 potato halves for Potato Dumplings. Make Potato Dumpling batter; set aside. Combine flour and water in small bowl; blend thoroughly. Add to saucepan; stir until thickened. Bring to a boil; drop dumpling batter by tablespoonfuls into saucepan. When dumplings rise to surface, cover pan. Reduce heat to medium low and cook 12 to 15 minutes. To serve, place 2 dumplings in each soup plate; ladle meat and sauce over top. Serve hot.

Grandma's Chicken Pie ——————— 6 to 8 servings

1 broiler-fryer (4 to 5 pounds), cut up
1 quart hot water
1 small onion, halved
1 stalk celery with leaves, cut into 3-inch pieces
3 sprigs parsley
1 1/2 teaspoons salt, divided
3 peppercorns
1 small bay leaf
4 medium potatoes, washed, peeled, and quartered
4 carrots, peeled and sliced
3 stalks celery, cut into 1-inch pieces
2 small onions, chopped
1/4 cup all-purpose flour
1/2 cup cold water
1 package (7.5 ounces) refrigerated buttermilk biscuit dough, separated

Place chicken pieces in 4-quart saucepan or Dutch oven. Add hot water, onion halves, celery stalk with leaves, parsley, 1 teaspoon salt, peppercorns, and bay leaf. Cover and bring to a boil; skim off foam. Replace cover and simmer 2 to 3 hours, or until chicken is tender. Remove chicken from broth; let cool until easily handled. Cut into bite-size pieces; set aside. Strain broth; cool; spoon off fat. Return broth to pan; bring to a boil. Add potatoes, carrots, celery, chopped onions and remaining 1/2 teaspoon salt. Cover and cook 20 minutes, or until vegetables are tender. Remove vegetables with slotted spoon. Place in deep 2-quart casserole. Arrange chicken over vegetables; set aside. Preheat oven to 425°F. Combine flour and cold water in small bowl; blend thoroughly. Stir into boiling broth. Cook until thickened, stirring constantly. Pour gravy over ingredients in casserole. Arrange biscuits on top with sides touching. Bake 15 to 20 minutes, or until biscuits are golden brown.

Lemony Tuna and Mashed Potatoes ———————— 6 servings

- 4 pieces lemon peel, cut into 1 × 1/2-inch strips
- 1 cup milk
- 2 tablespoons butter or margarine
- 2 tablespoons all-purpose flour
- 2 tablespoons mayonnaise
- 1 tablespoon lemon juice
- 1/4 teaspoon salt
- Dash pepper
- 1 can (9 1/4 ounces) tuna, drained and flaked
- 4 cups Mashed Potatoes (page 13)
- 1 tablespoon milk
- Paprika

Heat 1 cup milk in small saucepan; add lemon peel. Let stand about 20 minutes; strain; discard peel and reserve milk. Melt butter in 2-quart saucepan. Blend in flour. While stirring constantly, gradually add reserved milk; cook and stir until thickened. Blend in mayonnaise, lemon juice, salt, and pepper. Stir in tuna; set aside. Place potatoes and 1 tablespoon milk in separate saucepan; heat on moderate heat, stirring until hot. Reheat tuna mixture. Spoon potatoes around edge of serving dish. Spoon tuna mixture into center. Sprinkle with paprika.

For added flavor and color, 1/2 cup cooked peas or 1/4 cup sliced stuffed olives can be added to the tuna mixture, if desired.

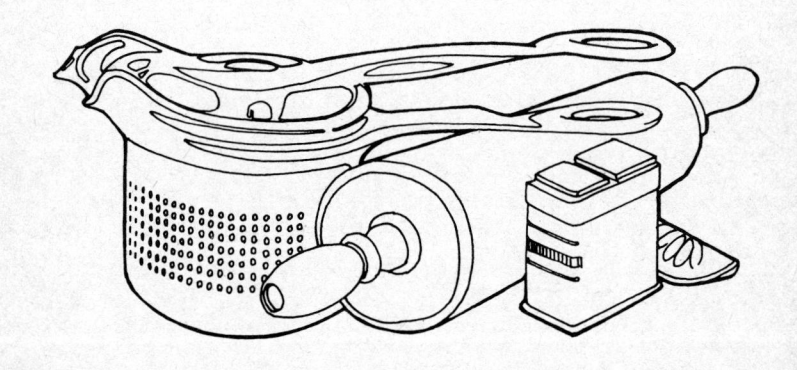

Crustless Tuna-Potato Quiche

6 servings

- 2 cups sliced cooked potatoes
- 1 can (12 1/2 ounces) chunk-style tuna, drained and flaked
- 2 cups (8 ounces) shredded Swiss cheese
- 1/2 cup sliced green onions
- 4 eggs, slightly beaten
- 2 cups half-and half
- 1/2 teaspoon dillweed
- 1/2 teaspoon salt
- 1/8 teaspoon pepper

Preheat oven to 325°F. Lightly grease a shallow 1 1/2-quart casserole. Arrange potatoes in prepared casserole. Spoon tuna over potatoes. Sprinkle with half of the cheese and half of the onion. Blend eggs, half-and-half, dillweed, salt, and pepper in small bowl. Pour carefully over ingredients in casserole. Sprinkle remaining cheese and onion evenly over top. Bake 45 minutes, or until set in center.

Clam-Potato Pie

6 servings

- 3 tablespoons butter or margarine
- 1/2 cup chopped onion
- 2 tablespoons all-purpose flour
- 1/2 teaspoon salt
- Dash white pepper
- 3 cans (7 1/2 ounces each) minced clams, drained, 1/2 cup liquid reserved
- 1/2 cup milk
- 2 large potatoes, washed, cooked, peeled, and diced
- 2 tablespoons minced parsley
- 1 9-inch pastry crust, unbaked

Preheat oven to 450°F. Heat butter in small skillet. Sauté onion until transparent. Blend in flour, salt, and pepper. While stirring, add reserved clam liquid and milk; cook until thickened, stirring constantly. Remove from heat. Stir in potatoes, clams, and parsley. Pour into 9-inch pie plate. Roll out pastry crust on lightly floured surface. Carefully place over ingredients in pie plate; flute edge. Cut slits in top of crust. Bake 20 minutes, or until pastry is golden brown. Serve hot.

Fish and Mushroom Ragout _____ 6 servings

- 1/4 cup butter or margarine
- 2 tablespoons all-purpose flour
- 1 1/4 teaspoons salt
- 1/4 teaspoon white pepper
- 1 cup milk
- 1 can (10 3/4 ounces) cream of tomato soup, undiluted
- 1 cup (4 ounces) shredded Cheddar cheese
- 1 1/4 pounds fresh, or frozen and thawed, sole or cod fillets
- 1/2 pound fresh mushrooms, sliced and sautéed
- 2 cups small potatoes, washed, cooked, peeled, and halved, or cubed large potatoes
- 1 can (8 ounces) small green peas, drained
- 1/8 teaspoon cayenne
- 1/3 cup cracker crumbs

Preheat oven to 375°F. Butter a 3-quart casserole; set aside. Melt butter in small saucepan. Add flour, salt, and pepper; cook 2 minutes, stirring constantly. Combine milk and soup in separate saucepan; heat through. Stir soup into flour; bring to a boil, stirring constantly. When smooth and thickened, stir in 1/2 cup cheese; stir until melted. Remove from heat. Carefully stir in fish, mushrooms, potatoes, peas, and cayenne. Pour into prepared casserole. Sprinkle with remaining cheese and cracker crumbs. Bake 20 minutes, or until hot and bubbly.

Humpty Dumpling and Friends

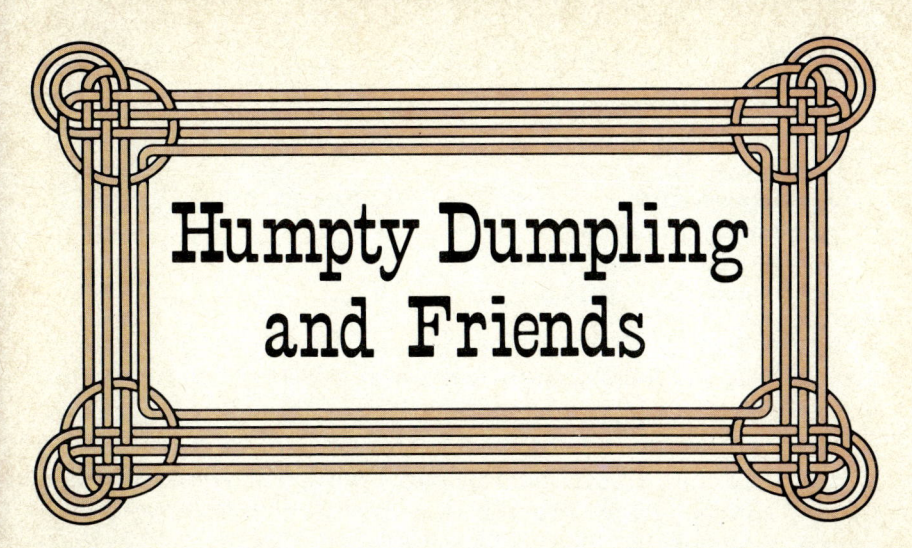

The recipes in this chapter can make "just another meal" into a banquet! Yes, there are dumplings and pancakes, and other traditional friends. But don't overlook Duchess Potatoes, Patrician Potatoes, Potato Soufflé, or Potato Stuffing. Looking for something new to brighten up your next party? Set up a Potato Bar!

Potato Soufflé
6 to 8 servings

- 4 medium potatoes, washed, cooked, and peeled
- 3 eggs, separated
- 1/2 teaspoon salt
- 1/4 teaspoon pepper
- 2 tablespoons dry bread crumbs
- 2 tablespoons parsley flakes
- 1/4 cup butter or margarine, melted

Preheat oven to 350°F. Lightly grease a 1 1/2-quart casserole; set aside. Mash potatoes in large bowl with electric mixer. Add egg yolks, salt, and pepper; mix well; set aside. Beat egg whites in separate bowl with electric mixer until stiff peaks form. Gently fold into potato mixture just until blended. Spoon into prepared casserole. Sprinkle bread crumbs and parsley on top. Drizzle butter evenly over top. Bake 25 to 30 minutes, or until top begins to brown. Serve immediately.

Spinach Pasta — 4 to 6 servings

- 3 cups all-purpose flour
- 1 cup Mashed Potatoes (page 13), at room temperature
- 1 package (10 ounces) frozen chopped spinach, cooked and drained
- 1 egg
- 3 teaspoons olive or vegetable oil
- 1/2 teaspoon salt

Combine flour, potatoes, spinach, egg, olive oil, and salt in large bowl or bowl of food processor fitted with steel blade; mix well. Add just enough water (about 1 to 2 tablespoons) to make a firm dough. (Dough will form a ball around center post of food processor.) Divide dough into 2 portions. Roll out, 1 portion at a time, on lightly floured surface, until very thin (or use pasta maker on widest setting, gradually working to lowest setting). Cut with sharp knife into 1/8-inch strips. Spread on lightly floured baking sheet; let dry, about 2 hours. Cook, following directions on page 69 for Potato Pasta, or store in airtight container.

Cauliflower-Potato Purée — 4 servings

- 1 large potato, washed peeled, and diced
- 3/4 teaspoon salt
- 1 package (8 ounces) frozen chopped cauliflower
- 1/4 cup milk
- 1 tablespoon butter or margarine
- 1/8 teaspoon nutmeg
- Parsley

Combine potato, 3/4 cup water, and salt in 1-quart saucepan; bring to a boil. Cover and cook on moderate heat 10 minutes, or until potato is tender. Add cauliflower; cover and bring to a boil. Boil 5 minutes, or until cauliflower is just tender; drain. Combine potato, cauliflower, milk, butter, and nutmeg in blender container or food processor fitted with steel blade; process until smooth. Spoon into serving dish. Garnish with parsley. Serve immediately.

Wine Potatoes ———————————————— 6 servings

- 6 large potatoes, washed peeled, and thinly sliced
- 1 teaspoon salt, divided
- 1/4 teaspoon pepper, divided
- 3/4 cup grated Cheddar cheese, divided
- 1/2 cup minced onion, divided
- 1 can (10 3/4 ounces) cream of mushroom soup, undiluted, divided
- 1/2 cup white wine, divided

Preheat oven to 400°F. Grease a 1 1/2-quart casserole. Arrange half of the potatoes on bottom. Sprinkle on half of the salt and pepper. Top with half of the cheese, onion, soup, and wine. Repeat layers with remaining ingredients. Cover and bake 1 hour, or until potatoes are tender. Remove cover and bake 10 minutes, or until top begins to brown. Serve hot.

Potato Pasta ———————————————— 4 servings

- 3 cups all-purpose flour
- 1 cup Mashed Potatoes (page 13), at room temperature
- 1 egg, slightly beaten
- 3 teaspoons olive or vegetable oil
- 1/2 teaspoon salt

Combine flour, potatoes, egg, olive oil, and salt in large bowl. Blend well, adding just enough water (about 1 to 2 tablespoons) to make a firm dough. Divide dough into 2 portions. Roll out, 1 portion at a time, on lightly floured surface, until very thin (or use pasta maker on widest setting, gradually working to lowest setting). Cut with sharp knife into 1/8-inch strips. Spread on lightly floured baking sheet; let dry, about 2 hours. Cook, following directions below, or store in airtight container.

To cook pasta, bring 4 1/2 quarts water to a boil in 6 to 8-quart saucepan. Add 1 teaspoon salt and 1 teaspoon olive oil. Shake excess flour from pasta. Drop pasta into boiling water. Cook 3 to 5 minutes, stirring constantly, until al dente (firm-tender). Drain; rinse in hot water. Return to saucepan; toss with 2 tablespoons butter. Serve immediately.

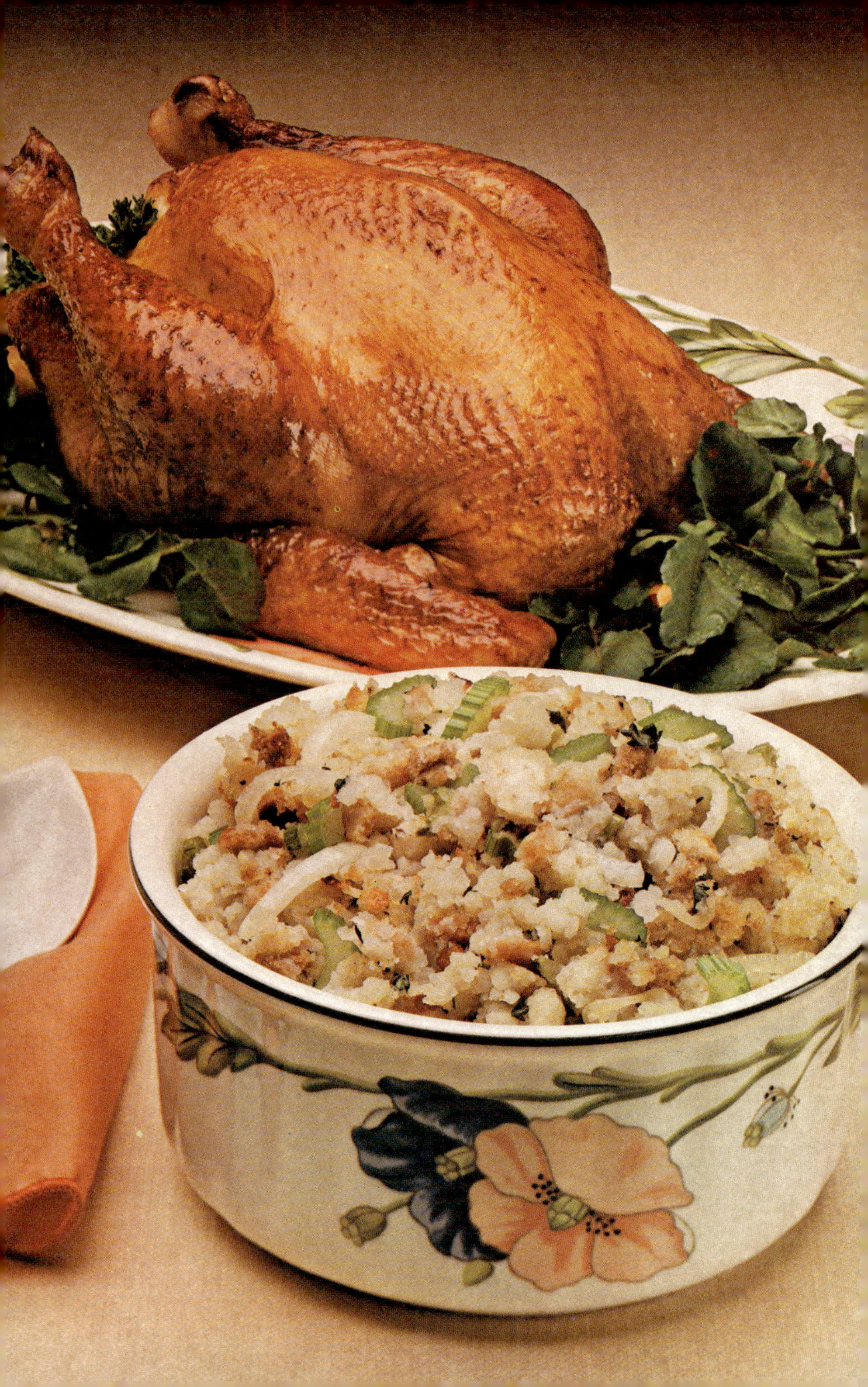

Potato Stuffing ——————————— 4 cups

- 2 cups Mashed Potatoes (page 13)
- 1 cup coarse dry bread crumbs
- 1/2 cup chopped celery
- 1/4 cup chopped onion
- 4 tablespoons butter or margarine, melted
- 2 tablespoons onion juice
- 1 teaspoon sage
- 1/2 teaspoon summer savory
- 1/2 teaspoon salt
- 1/2 teaspoon pepper

Combine all ingredients in large bowl; blend thoroughly. To serve as a side dish, preheat oven to 350°F. Butter a 2-quart casserole. Spoon mixture into prepared casserole. Bake 1 hour, or until heated through. To stuff goose, duck, or roasting chicken, lightly spoon stuffing into cavity. Bake as directed for individual bird.

Country-Style Potato Pancakes ——————————— 4 servings

- 2 eggs, slightly beaten
- 2 large potatoes, washed, peeled, and grated
- 2 medium onions, grated
- 1 1/2 tablespoons all-purpose flour
- 1 teaspoon baking powder
- 1 tablespoon chopped parsley
- 1/2 teaspoon salt
- 1/4 teaspoon white pepper

Combine all ingredients in large bowl; mix well. Form potato mixture into 8 patties. Lightly grease large skillet. Add patties and cook on moderate heat 4 minutes, or until golden brown. Turn and cook 4 to 5 minutes, or until potatoes are cooked and pancakes are golden brown. Serve hot; pass maple syrup or applesauce, if desired.

Potato Stuffing

Patrician Potatoes ———————————— 12 servings

- 6 medium Basic Baked Potatoes (page 14), warm
- 1 cup cream-style cottage cheese
- 1 cup dairy sour cream
- 2 tablespoons chopped green onion
- 2 tablespoons butter or margarine
- 1/2 teaspoon salt
- 1/4 teaspoon pepper
- 1/4 cup Parmesan cheese
- 1/2 cup toasted blanched almonds

Cut potatoes in half lengthwise; carefully remove all pulp; place in medium bowl; mash with fork. Add cottage cheese, sour cream, onion, butter, salt, and pepper. Stir until thoroughly blended. Fill potato shells with potato mixture. Sprinkle cheese and almonds over each potato. Broil, 5 inches from heat, 3 to 4 minutes, or until potatoes are hot and cheese has melted. Serve immediately.

Potatoes on the Grill ———————————— 3 servings

- 3 medium potatoes, washed, peeled, and thinly sliced
- 1 small onion, peeled and sliced
- 1/4 cup butter or margarine
- 1/2 teaspoon salt (optional)
- 1/4 teaspoon pepper (optional)

Place potatoes and onion on double thickness of aluminum foil. Dot with butter. Sprinkle with salt and pepper, if desired. Wrap tightly. Cook on grill over direct heat about 1 hour, or until tender, turning potatoes over halfway through cooking.

Grill fans will also enjoy this variation. Cut washed potatoes into 1-inch thick slices. Dip in melted butter or margarine. Sprinkle with salt, if desired. Brown on grill. Move potatoes to edge away from coals. Cover and grill over indirect heat about 20 minutes.

Onion-Potato Bake ———————— 4 to 6 servings

- 3 medium onions, peeled and thinly sliced
- 2 medium potatoes, washed, peeled, and thinly sliced
- 1/2 teaspoon salt, divided
- 1/4 teaspoon pepper, divided
- 1/2 cup milk
- 2 tablespoons chopped pimiento
- 2 tablespoons parsley flakes
- 1/2 cup shredded Swiss cheese

Preheat oven to 350°F. Grease a 1 1/2-quart casserole. Layer half the onion and potato slices on bottom of casserole. Sprinkle with half the salt and pepper. Combine milk, pimiento, and parsley in 1-cup measure. Pour half of the milk mixture over onions and potatoes. Repeat layers with remaining ingredients. Cover with aluminum foil. Bake 1 hour, or until potatoes are tender. Remove foil. Sprinkle cheese evenly over top. Bake 10 minutes, or until cheese is melted. Serve hot.

Heidelberg Casserole ———————— 8 to 10 servings

- 8 cups Mashed Potatoes (page 13), at room temperature
- 1 package (8 ounces) cream cheese, softened
- 1 container (8 ounces) dairy sour cream
- 1/2 cup butter or margarine, at room temperature
- 1 clove garlic, minced
- 1/4 teaspoon salt
- 1/2 cup grated Cheddar cheese

Preheat oven to 350°F. Lightly grease a 9 × 13-inch baking dish; set aside. Combine potatoes, cream cheese, sour cream, butter, garlic, and salt in large bowl; beat with electric mixer until smooth. Spoon into prepared baking dish. Sprinkle cheese evenly over top. Bake 1 hour to 1 hour 15 minutes, or until heated through and cheese is golden brown. Serve hot.

Potato-Broccoli Bake ——————— 4 servings

- 3 large potatoes, washed, peeled, and thinly sliced
- 1 package (10 ounces) frozen broccoli spears
- 3 tablespoons butter or margarine
- 3 tablespoons all-purpose flour
- 1 cup milk, heated
- 1 teaspoon salt
- 1/4 teaspoon pepper
- 1/4 teaspoon paprika
- 1 jar (4 ounces) diced pimientos, drained
- 1 cup shredded Cheddar cheese

Preheat oven to 375°F. Grease an 8-inch square baking pan. Arrange potatoes on bottom of pan. Arrange broccoli spears on top of potatoes; set aside. Melt butter in small saucepan on moderate heat. Add flour; while stirring constantly, gradually add milk. Cook just until thickened. Add salt, pepper, and paprika. Pour over vegetables in pan. Sprinkle with pimientos and cheese. Cover with aluminum foil. Bake 45 to 50 minutes, or until potatoes are tender. Serve hot.

Baked Potato Halves ——————— 12 servings

- 6 medium potatoes, washed; do not peel
- 1/2 cup butter or margarine, melted
- 1 cup cracker crumbs
- 2 tablespoons grated Parmesan cheese

Preheat oven to 350°F. Cut potatoes in half lengthwise. Dip cut sides into melted butter, then into cracker crumbs. Place, skin-side down, on baking sheet. Sprinkle with cheese. Bake 40 to 45 minutes, or until tender. Serve warm.

Small potatoes can also be prepared this way: for 6 small potatoes, reduce baking time to 30 minutes. Or, potatoes can be cut crosswise into 1/4-inch slices. Arrange directly on oven rack. Bake at 425°F 20 minutes. Sprinkle with salt, if desired. Serve with melted butter as dippers.

Duchess Potatoes ——————— 4 to 6 servings

    4 large potatoes, washed, cooked, and peeled
    1/2 cup butter or margarine
    1/2 teaspoon salt
    1/4 teaspoon pepper
    1 egg yolk

Combine potatoes, butter, salt, and pepper in top of double boiler. Beat with electric mixer until smooth. Place top over simmering water. Cook, stirring constantly, 5 to 7 minutes, or until potatoes are very hot. Stir in egg yolk; cook 5 minutes. Serve hot.

You can use Duchess Potatoes to garnish serving platters. Pipe warm potatoes through pastry bag fitted with medium star tip onto a lightly oiled baking sheet. Place in preheated 400°F oven 15 minutes, or until lightly browned. Remove from baking sheet. Arrange potatoes around edge of platter. Potatoes can also be piped directly onto an ovenproof platter and browned.

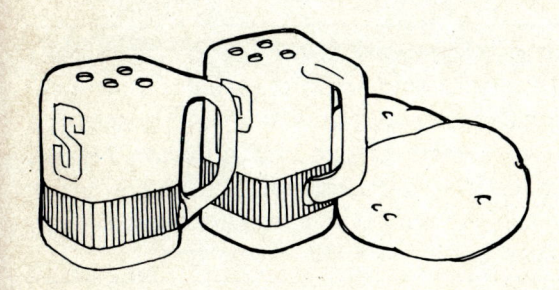

Potatoes Anna ——————— 6 servings

    4 large potatoes, washed, peeled, and thinly sliced
    4 tablespoons butter or margarine, melted, divided
    1 teaspoon salt, divided
    1/2 teaspoon freshly ground pepper, divided

Preheat oven to 425°F. Generously grease a 10-inch pie plate. Beginning in center of pie plate, arrange potatoes in circles to edge of plate, overlapping slices. Pour 1 tablespoon butter over potatoes. Sprinkle on 1/4 teaspoon salt, and 1/8 teaspoon pepper. Repeat layers with remaining ingredients. Cover with aluminum foil. Bake 50 minutes, or until potatoes are tender and golden brown. Drain butter. Carefully turn potatoes upside down onto serving plate. Serve immediately.

Potatoes Basil
_____ 4 servings

- 1/2 small onion, finely chopped
- 1 small clove garlic, crushed
- 2 tablespoons Italian dressing
- 3 medium potatoes, washed, peeled, and cut into 1-inch cubes
- 1/2 green pepper, seeded and chopped
- 1 cup cherry tomatoes, halved
- 1/2 teaspoon salt
- 1 tablespoon chopped fresh basil or 3/4 teaspoon dried basil

Combine onion, garlic, and salad dressing in small skillet. Cook on moderate heat 5 minutes, or until onion is transparent. Add potatoes and 1/2 cup water. Cover and cook on low heat 10 minutes. Cover and cook on low heat 15 minutes, or until potatoes and green pepper are tender. Stir in tomatoes, salt, and basil. Cover and cook 5 minutes, or until tomatoes are heated through. Serve hot.

To prepare this recipe in a microwave oven, use a round glass casserole. Combine onion, garlic, and salad dressing. Cover with plastic wrap. Cook on High 2 minutes, or until onion is transparent. Add potatoes and 1/4 cup water. Cover and cook on High 5 minutes. Add green pepper; stir. Cover and cook 5 minutes. Stir in tomatoes, salt, and basil. Cover and cook 1 minute. Let stand on heatproof surface 2 minutes before serving. Serve hot.

Potatoes Basil, Potatoes Anna (page 75)

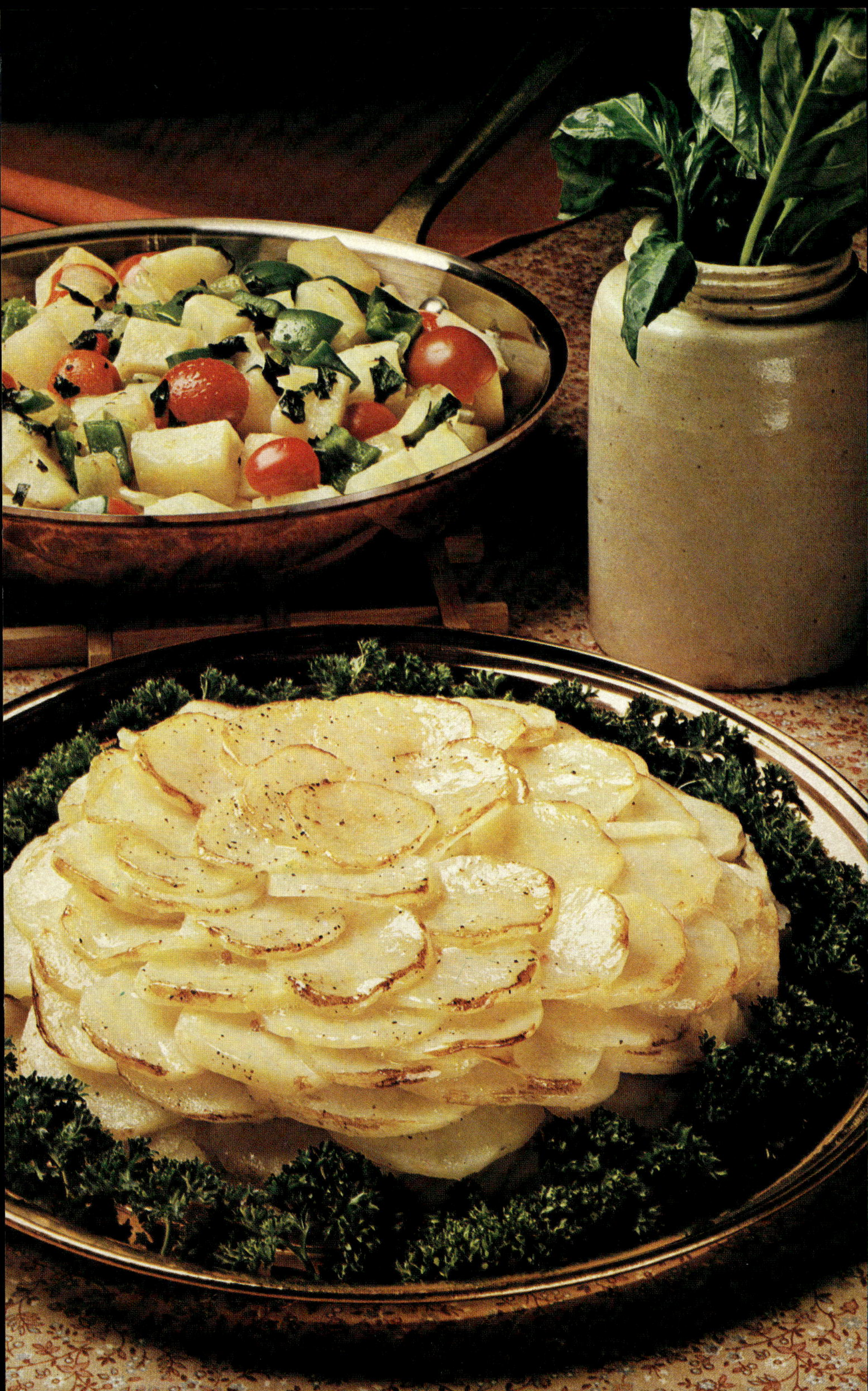

Fluffy Apple-Potato Pancakes

6 to 8 servings

- 3 large potatoes, washed peeled, and grated
- 2 large tart apples, peeled, cored, and grated
- 1 small onion, grated
- 3 eggs, separated
- 1 1/4 cups all-purpose flour
- 1/2 teaspoon salt

Combine potatoes, apples, onion, egg yolks, flour, and salt in large bowl; blend well. Beat egg whites in small bowl with electric mixer until stiff peaks form. Gently fold whites into potato mixture just until blended. Lightly grease electric griddle or large skillet; set heat at 375°F or medium high. Pour about 1/4 cup of the batter onto hot griddle; cook about 3 minutes, or until golden brown. Turn and cook 3 to 4 minutes, or until potatoes are cooked and pancakes are golden brown. Keep hot. Repeat with remaining batter. Serve hot with butter.

Boston Baked Potatoes

6 servings

- 4 medium potatoes, washed peeled, and thinly sliced
- 3 slices bacon, diced
- 1 medium onion, chopped
- 1/4 cup vinegar
- 1/4 cup light molasses
- 1/4 cup firmly packed brown sugar
- 1 teaspoon dry mustard
- 1 teaspoon salt

Preheat oven to 375°F. Combine potatoes, bacon, onion, vinegar, molasses, sugar, mustard, and salt in greased 2-quart casserole; toss carefully just to mix. Bake, covered, 45 to 50 minutes, or until potatoes are tender.

To prepare this recipe in a microwave oven, follow above directions using approved microwave casserole. Cover with plastic wrap. Cook on High 10 minutes. Uncover and stir. Cook, uncovered, 5 minutes. Let stand 5 minutes before serving.

Delmonico Potatoes ——————— 4 to 6 servings

- 2 tablespoons butter or margarine
- 2 tablespoons all-purpose flour
- 1 cup milk, heated
- 1/2 teaspoon salt
- 1/4 teaspoon white pepper
- 3 large potatoes, washed, cooked, and peeled
- 3 hard-cooked eggs, sliced
- 1/2 cup grated Cheddar cheese

Preheat oven to 350°F. Grease a 1 1/2-quart casserole; set aside. Melt butter in small saucepan on moderate heat. Add flour; stir constantly for 2 minutes. While stirring constantly, gradually add milk. Cook just until thickened. Remove from heat. Stir in salt and pepper; set aside. Cut potatoes into thin slices. Layer potatoes, eggs, and cheese in prepared casserole. Pour sauce over ingredients in casserole. Cover with aluminum foil. Bake 15 to 20 minutes, or until heated through.

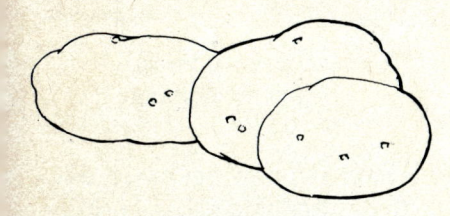

Party Potatoes ——————— 8 to 10 servings

- 8 large Basic Baked Potatoes (page 14), hot
- 1/2 pound sharp Cheddar cheese, grated (2 cups)
- 1 pint dairy sour cream
- 1 cup thinly sliced green onion
- 1 teaspoon salt
- 1/4 teaspoon pepper
- 2 tablespoons minced parsley

Preheat oven to 350°F. Lightly grease a 3-quart soufflé or straight-sided baking dish. While potatoes are hot, cut in half lengthwise; carefully remove all pulp. (Use skins for Twice-Baked Potato Skins, page 24). Combine potato pulp and cheese in large bowl; beat until smooth. Add sour cream, onion, salt, and pepper. Spoon into prepared dish. Bake, uncovered, 40 minutes, or until puffed and lightly browned. Garnish with parsley. Serve hot.

Potato Bar

Surround Basic Baked Potatoes (page 14), with bowls of any of the following or use your imagination:

- Chopped red onion
- Bacon-flavored bits or crumbled crisp bacon
- Chopped parsley
- Chopped green pepper
- Shredded Cheddar or Swiss cheese
- Crumbled blue cheese
- Grated Parmesan cheese
- Sliced radishes
- Alfalfa sprouts
- Sliced stuffed olives
- Sliced almonds
- Sliced or chopped fresh mushrooms
- Dairy sour cream
- Chives
- Applesauce
- Lemon-butter sauce
- Sour cream and horseradish sauce
- Yogurt
- Butter or margarine
- Salt
- Freshly ground pepper
- Mock Sour Cream (below)

Dollar Potatoes ─────────── 4 servings

- 2 large potatoes, washed; do not peel
- 1/4 cup butter or margarine
- 2 green onions, thinly sliced; include part of top

Preheat oven to 425°F. Butter a 4×8-inch loaf pan; set aside. Slice potatoes crosswise, about 3/16-inch thick, keeping slices in order. Carefully arrange potatoes in prepared loaf pan. Melt butter in small saucepan; stir in onion. Pour over potatoes. Bake, uncovered, 1 hour, or until potatoes are tender. Turn out onto heated plate to serve.

Mock Sour Cream ─────────── 1 1/4 cups

- 1 tablespoon lemon juice
- 1 cup cream-style cottage cheese
- 1/4 teaspoon salt (optional)

Place all ingredients in blender container with 1/4 cup water. Blend on high speed about 10 seconds, or until completely smooth.

Cold Mock Sour Cream can be substituted in any recipe calling for dairy sour cream.

Potato-Celery Casserole ———— 4 to 6 servings

- 5 medium potatoes, washed peeled, and thinly sliced
- 1 can (10 3/4 ounces) cream of celery soup, undiluted
- 3/4 cup milk
- 1/2 cup sliced celery
- 1 medium onion, chopped
- 1 tablespoon parsley flakes
- 1/2 teaspoon salt
- 1/4 teaspoon pepper
- 1/4 cup shredded Cheddar cheese

Preheat oven to 350°F. Grease an 8-inch square pan. Arrange potatoes on bottom. Combine soup, milk, celery, onion, parsley, salt, and pepper in medium bowl; blend well. Pour soup mixture over potatoes. Sprinkle cheese evenly over top. Cover with aluminum foil. Bake 45 minutes, or until potatoes are tender. Serve hot.

Scalloped Potatoes ———— 4 to 6 servings

- 3 medium potatoes, washed, peeled, and sliced
- 3/4 teaspoon Italian herb seasoning
- 1/2 teaspoon salt
- 1/2 teaspoon instant beef bouillon granules
- 1/8 teaspoon pepper
- 2 tablespoons butter or margarine
- 1/2 cup grated Cheddar cheese
- 2 tablespoons grated Parmesan cheese
- 1/4 teaspoon paprika

Preheat oven to 350°F. Grease an 8-inch round baking dish. Arrange potatoes on bottom of dish. Combine 1/2 cup water, Italian seasoning, salt, bouillon, and pepper in small bowl; pour over potatoes. Dot with butter. Cover with aluminum foil. Bake 40 to 45 minutes, or until potatoes are tender. Remove foil. Sprinkle with cheeses and paprika. Bake, uncovered, 8 to 10 minutes, or until cheeses are melted. Serve hot.

To prepare this recipe in a microwave oven, use an approved microwave casserole. Prepare potatoes as directed above. Cover with plastic wrap. Cook on High 4 minutes. Stir; cook on High 4 minutes. Sprinkle with cheeses and paprika; cook on High 2 minutes. Let stand on heatproof surface 5 minutes before serving.

Potato Dumplings — 6 servings

1 medium potato, washed, cooked, and peeled
1 egg, slightly beaten
1/4 cup all-purpose flour
1 tablespoon minced parsley
1/2 teaspoon salt
1/4 teaspoon pepper

Mash potato with fork in small bowl. Add egg, flour, parsley, salt, and pepper; blend well. Bring 6 cups water to a boil in large saucepan. Drop batter by tablespoonfuls into boiling water. When dumplings rise to surface, reduce heat to medium low; cover and simmer 12 to 15 minutes.

Potato Dumplings can also be cooked in soups and stews instead of water. See also Chicken Fricassee (page 62).

Creamed Potatoes — 4 servings

4 medium potatoes, washed, peeled, and cubed
1 cup half-and-half or milk
2 tablespoons butter or margarine
1 teaspoon chopped chives
1 teaspoon parsley flakes
1/2 teaspoon salt
1/4 teaspoon pepper
1/4 teaspoon nutmeg

Combine all ingredients in 1 1/2-quart saucepan; stir to blend. Cover and simmer 12 to 15 minutes, or just until potatoes are tender. Do not boil. Serve hot.

Potato Dumplings, Chicken Fricassee (page 62)

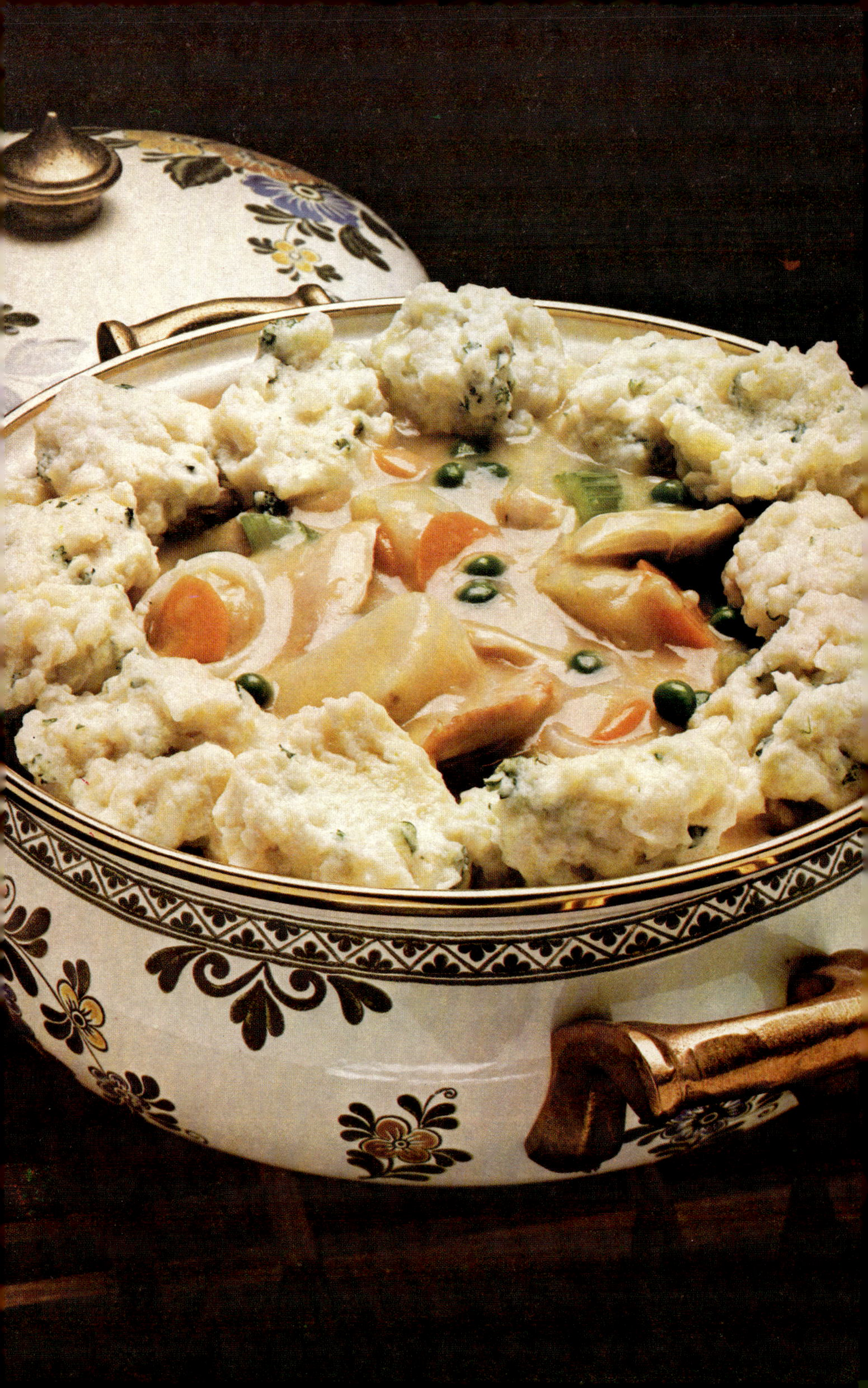

Mashed Potato Casserole ———— 4 to 6 servings

- 4 cups Mashed Potatoes (page 13), at room temperature
- 1 package (8 ounces) cream cheese, softened
- 1 egg
- 1/2 cup finely chopped onion

Preheat oven to 350°F. Lightly grease a 2-quart casserole; set aside. Combine potatoes, cream cheese, and egg in large bowl; beat with electric mixer until smooth. Stir in onion. Spoon into prepared casserole. Bake 1 hour, or until heated through. Serve hot.

Creamy Paprika Potatoes ———— 6 servings

- 2 tablespoons butter or margarine
- 1/4 cup chopped onion
- 2 tablespoons all-purpose flour
- 1 teaspoon paprika
- 1/4 teaspoon salt
- 1 can (10 1/2 ounces) chicken broth, heated
- 1 cup dairy sour cream
- 2 tablespoons tomato paste
- 5 medium potatoes, washed, cooked, peeled, and diced

Melt butter in large skillet. Sauté onion until limp. Stir in flour, paprika, and salt. While stirring constantly, gradually add broth. Cook and stir until slightly thickened. Remove from heat. Combine sour cream and tomato paste in small bowl. Stir sour cream mixture, 1/4 cup at a time, into mixture in skillet. Gently stir in diced potatoes. Cook on low heat, stirring gently, 3 to 5 minutes, or until heated through.

The Meal in a Peel

Butter and sour cream (maybe topped with chives) have long been standard baked potato toppings. True blue potato lovers, however, realized that the potato was destined for greater things. Here's their baked potato breakthrough — the Meal in a Peel! For breakfast: Creamed Chipped Beef. For lunch: Seafood Thermidor. Dinner? Spaghetti Supreme. From easy to elegant, these recipes are sure to please even the most dyed-in-the-wool baked-potato-and-sour-cream fan.

Baked Potatoes-Bacon-Eggs — 4 servings

- 1/2 pound bacon
- 1/2 cup chopped onion
- 2 tablespoons all-purpose flour
- 3/4 teaspoon dry mustard
- Dash pepper
- 2 cups milk, heated
- 3 hard-cooked eggs, sliced
- 1 tablespoon minced parsley
- 4 Basic Baked Potatoes (page 14), hot

Fry bacon in skillet until crisp. Remove with slotted spoon; drain on paper towels; crumble. Set aside. Pour off all but 2 tablespoons drippings from skillet. Add onion; sauté until tender. Stir flour, mustard, and pepper into drippings in skillet until smooth. While stirring constantly, gradually add milk. Cook and stir until thickened. Carefully stir in eggs, parsley, and bacon. Open potatoes; fluff insides with fork. Divide and spoon egg mixture over each potato.

Creamed Chipped Beef ———— 4 servings

- 2 jars (2 1/2 ounces each) sliced dried beef
- 3/4 cup boiling water
- 1/4 cup butter or margarine
- 1 tablespoon minced green onion
- 1/4 cup all-purpose flour
- 1 cup chicken broth, heated
- 3/4 cup heavy cream
- 1/2 teaspoon prepared mustard
- 1/4 teaspoon ginger
- Dash hot pepper sauce
- 2 tablespoons sherry
- 4 Basic Baked Potatoes (page 14), hot
- Minced parsley

Combine beef and boiling water in small bowl; let stand 5 minutes. Drain; chop beef. Melt butter in 2-quart saucepan on moderate heat. Add green onion; saute 3 minutes, or until golden, stirring frequently. Stir in flour; cook and stir 2 minutes. While stirring constantly, gradually add broth. Cook and stir until thickened. Reduce heat to low; stir in beef, cream, mustard, ginger, and hot pepper sauce; cook and stir 2 minutes. Stir in sherry. Open potatoes; fluff insides with fork. Divide and spoon beef mixture over each potato. Sprinkle with parsley.

To prepare this recipe in a microwave oven, prepare beef as directed above. Cook potatoes in microwave oven according to directions on page 14. Place butter and green onion in 1-quart glass measure. Cook, uncovered, on High 2 minutes. Blend in flour. Cook on High 1 minute. Stir in broth and cream. Cook on High 2 minutes, beating every 30 seconds until thickened. Stir in beef, mustard, 1/8 teaspoon ginger, hot pepper sauce and sherry. If mixture is not hot enough, reheat on High 30 seconds. Serve as directed above.

South-of-the-Border Topping ———— 2 servings

- 1/2 pound lean ground beef
- 1/2 cup taco sauce
- 1 cup shredded Cheddar cheese
- 1/3 cup crushed corn chips
- 2 Basic Baked Potatoes (page 14), hot

Sauté ground beef until brown in small skillet; drain fat. Stir taco sauce into beef. Open potatoes; fluff insides with fork. Spoon half of the mixture over each potato. Sprinkle with cheese and chips. Serve with additional taco sauce, if desired.

Mushroom and Wine Topper —— 2 servings

- 2 tablespoons butter or margarine
- 2 tablespoons all-purpose flour
- 3/4 cup chicken broth, heated
- 1/4 teaspoon salt
- Dash white pepper
- 2 tablespoons dry white wine
- 1 cup sliced fresh mushrooms
- 1/2 cup dairy sour cream
- 2 Basic Baked Potatoes (page 14), hot
- 2 tablespoons grated Parmesan cheese

Melt butter in small saucepan on moderate heat. Add flour; blend well. While stirring constantly, gradually add broth. Add salt and pepper; stir until thickened. Stir in wine. Add mushrooms; simmer until mushrooms are tender, stirring occasionally. Stir in sour cream; heat through, stirring frequently; do not boil. Open potatoes; fluff insides with fork. Divide and spoon mushroom mixture over each potato. Sprinkle with cheese.

One can (4 ounces) mushroom pieces can be substitited for sliced fresh mushrooms.

Savory Fish —— 4 servings

- 2 tablespoons butter or margarine
- 1/2 cup chopped onion
- 2 tablespoons all-purpose flour
- 1 1/2 cups milk
- 1/2 teaspoon dillweed
- 1 teaspoon lemon juice
- 1/2 teaspoon salt
- 1/4 teaspoon white pepper
- 1 tablespoon capers
- 1 pound fish fillets, cooked and cut into bite-size pieces
- 4 Basic Baked Potatoes (page 14), hot
- Minced parsley

Melt butter in 3-quart saucepan on moderate heat. Sauté onion until limp. Stir in flour; blend well. While stirring constantly, gradually add milk; stir until thickened. Add dillweed, lemon juice, salt, pepper, and capers. Carefully stir in fish; heat through. Open potatoes; fluff insides with fork. Divide and spoon fish mixture over each potato. Sprinkle with parsley.

Beef Stroganoff _____ 8 servings

- 2 pounds lean ground beef
- 1 teaspoon salt
- 1/4 teaspoon pepper
- 4 teaspoons bottled steak sauce
- 1/3 cup fine dry bread crumbs
- 1 egg
- 4 tablespoons butter or margarine, divided
- 1/2 pound fresh mushrooms, sliced
- 2 tablespoons all-purpose flour
- 1 tablespoon catsup
- 1 teaspoon Worcestershire sauce
- 1 can (10 1/2 ounces) beef broth
- 1/2 package (1 5/8 ounces) dry onion soup mix
- 1 cup dairy sour cream
- 8 Basic Baked Potatoes (page 14), hot
- Paprika

Combine beef, salt, pepper, steak sauce, bread crumbs, and egg in large bowl; blend well. Gently shape into 1/2-inch balls. Melt 2 tablespoons butter in large skillet on moderate heat. Brown meatballs on all sides. Reduce heat to low; cook 10 minutes. With slotted spoon, remove meatballs; set aside. Add remaining 2 tablespoons butter to drippings in skillet. Raise heat to moderate; add mushrooms; sauté until tender, stirring occasionally. Stir in flour, catsup, and Worcestershire. Add broth and onion soup mix; stir constantly until thickened. Reduce heat to low; simmer 2 minutes. Add meatballs; heat through. Stir in sour cream; heat through but do not boil. Open potatoes; fluff insides with fork. Spoon stroganoff mixture over each potato. Sprinkle with paprika. Serve hot.

Broccoli-Ham Sling _____ 2 servings

- 1 package (10 ounces) frozen cut broccoli in cheese sauce, prepared according to package directions
- 1 cup diced cooked ham
- 1/4 cup shredded Cheddar cheese
- 2 Basic Baked Potatoes (page 14), hot

Combine broccoli and ham in small saucepan; heat through. Open potatoes; fluff insides with fork. Divide and spoon broccoli-ham mixture over each potato. Sprinkle with cheese. Serve hot.

Guacamole Topping ———————— 6 servings

- 2 ripe avocados, peeled, pitted, and sliced
- 1 medium tomato, peeled, seeded, and chopped
- 1/4 cup minced canned mild or hot green chilies
- 1 1/2 tablespoons lemon juice
- 1/2 teaspoon salt
- 6 Basic Baked Potatoes (page 14), hot
- 2 tablespoons bacon-flavored bits

Mash avocados in medium bowl with potato masher or fork. Blend in tomato, chilies, lemon juice, and salt. Open potatoes; fluff insides with fork. Divide and spoon avocado mixture over each potato. Sprinkle with bacon bits.

This is also excellent as a dip for chips. Recipe makes 2 cups dip. Bacon-flavored bits can be eliminated, if desired.

Spaghetti Supreme ———————— 6 servings

- 2 tablespoons olive oil
- 1 medium onion, chopped
- 1 clove garlic, minced
- 1 can (4 ounces) mushroom bits and pieces, drained
- 1 pound lean ground beef
- 1 can (16 ounces) whole tomatoes, undrained
- 1 can (6 ounces) tomato paste
- 1 teaspoon salt
- 1/2 teaspoon oregano
- 1/4 teaspoon pepper
- 2 tablespoons vermouth
- 6 Basic Baked Potatoes (page 14), hot
- Grated Parmesan cheese

Heat olive oil in 3-quart saucepan. Sauté onion and garlic until onion is transparent. Add mushrooms and beef; cook 10 minutes, or until beef is no longer red, stirring to break up beef. Drain fat. Stir in tomatoes with liquid, tomato paste, salt, oregano, and pepper; break up tomatoes with spoon. Bring to a boil; cover and simmer 2 hours. Stir in vermouth. Open potatoes; fluff insides with fork. Divide and spoon meat sauce over each potato. Sprinkle with cheese. Serve hot.

Golden Creamy Chipped Beef —— 6 servings

- 3 jars (2 1/2 ounces each) sliced dried beef
- 3 tablespoons butter or margarine
- 3 tablespoons all-purpose flour
- 2 cups warm milk
- 1/2 cup golden raisins
- 1/2 teaspoon curry powder
- 6 Basic Baked Potatoes (page 14), hot

Pull beef apart into bite-size pieces; if very salty, rinse; set aside. Melt butter in small saucepan on moderate heat. Stir in flour; blend well. While stirring constantly, gradually add milk. Add beef; simmer until thickened. Stir in raisins and curry powder. Open potatoes; fluff insides with fork. Divide and spoon sauce over potatoes.

Chili-Cheddar Topping —————— 6 servings

- 1 1/2 pounds lean ground beef
- 1/2 cup chopped onion
- 1/2 cup chopped green pepper
- 1 clove garlic, minced
- 2 cans (8 ounces each) tomato sauce
- 1/2 cup chili sauce
- 2 tablespoons chili powder
- 1/2 teaspoon salt
- 1/4 teaspoon cumin
- 6 Basic Baked Potatoes (page 14), hot
- 1 cup Cheddar cheese, shredded

Combine ground beef, onion, green pepper, and garlic in 10-inch skillet. Cook until beef is no longer red, stirring to break up beef; drain fat. Stir in tomato sauce, chili sauce, chili powder, salt, and cumin; simmer 20 minutes. Open potatoes; fluff insides with fork. Divide and spoon chili mixture over each potato. Sprinkle with cheese. Serve hot.

To prepare this recipe in a microwave oven, use a 3-quart glass casserole. Combine beef, onion, green pepper and garlic. Cook on High 8 minutes, or until beef is no longer red and vegetables are tender, stirring after 4 minutes; drain. Stir in remaining ingredients, except potatoes and cheese. Cook on High 7 minutes, stirring after 4 minutes. Serve as directed above.

Golden Creamy Chipped Beef, Chili-Cheddar Topping, Shrimp-Mushroom Topper (page 92)

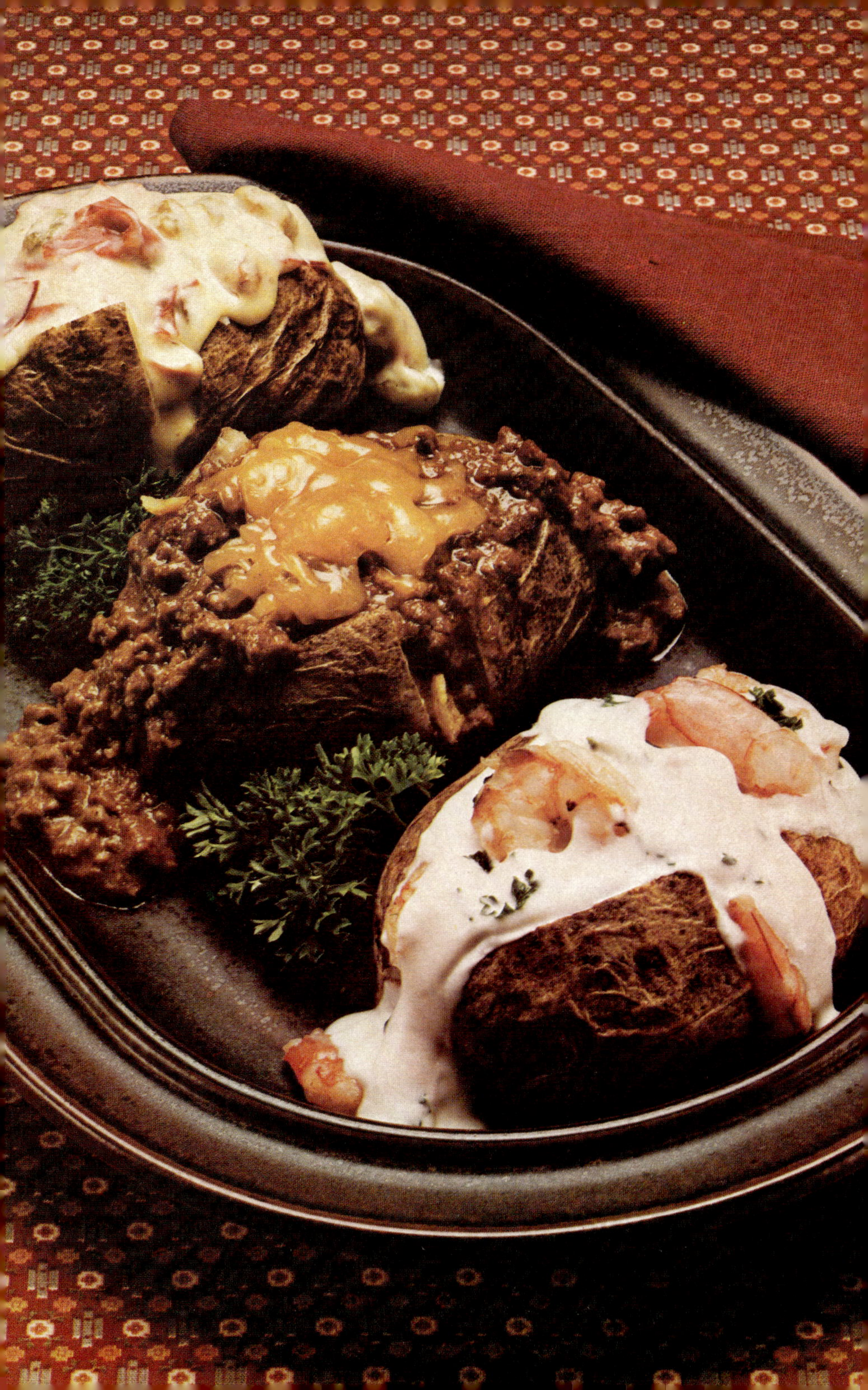

Shrimp-Mushroom Topper ———— 4 servings

- 4 tablespoons butter or margarine
- 1/2 pound fresh mushrooms, quartered
- 2 tablespoons minced parsley
- 1 teaspoon caraway seed
- 1/2 teaspoon salt
- 1/2 pound medium shrimp, cooked, shelled, and deveined
- 1 cup dairy sour cream
- 2 tablespoons sherry (optional)
- 4 Basic Baked Potatoes (page 14), hot

Melt butter in saucepan. Sauté mushrooms and parsley until mushrooms are tender. Sprinkle with caraway seed and salt. Stir in shrimp; heat through. Stir in sour cream and sherry; heat through, stirring frequently; do not boil. Open potatoes; fluff insides with fork. Divide and spoon shrimp-mushroom mixture over each potato.

Northern Italian Meat Sauce ———— 6 servings

- 2 tablespoons vegetable oil
- 3 medium carrots, finely chopped
- 1 stalk celery, finely chopped
- 1 small onion, finely chopped
- 3 cups shredded cooked roast beef
- 1 can (10 1/2 ounces) beef broth
- 1 can (6 ounces) tomato paste
- 1/2 cup dry red wine
- 1 teaspoon sugar
- 1 teaspoon salt
- 1/4 teaspoon pepper
- 1/2 cup heavy cream
- 6 Basic Baked Potatoes (page 14), hot
- Minced parsley

Heat oil in 3-quart saucepan on moderate heat. Add carrots, celery, and onion; cook, stirring occasionally, until tender. Stir in beef, broth, tomato paste, wine, sugar, salt, and pepper. Simmer 30 minutes, or until slightly thickened, stirring occasionally. Stir in cream; heat through. Open potatoes; fluff insides with fork. Divide and spoon beef mixture over each potato. Sprinkle with parsley.

Creamed Ham and Peas ———— 6 servings

- 1/3 cup butter or margarine
- 1/2 cup chopped onion
- 6 tablespoons all-purpose flour
- 1/2 teaspoon dry mustard
- 1/8 teaspoon pepper
- 3 1/2 cups milk, heated
- 1 package (8 ounces) cream cheese, cubed
- 1 package (10 ounces) frozen peas, prepared according to package directions
- 3 cups cubed cooked ham
- 1 can (4 ounces) sliced mushrooms, drained
- 1/2 teaspoon Worcestershire sauce
- 6 Basic Baked Potatoes (page 14), hot
- 2 tablespoons minced parsley

Melt butter in 3-quart saucepan on moderate heat. Sauté onion until tender, but do not brown. Stir flour, mustard, and pepper into drippings until smooth. While stirring constantly, gradually add milk. Cook and stir until mixture thickens. Reduce heat to low. Add cream cheese; stir until melted. Drain peas; add ham, peas, mushrooms, and Worcestershire to sauce mixture. Cook, stirring occasionally, until heated through. Open potatoes; fluff insides with fork. Divide and spoon ham-peas mixture over each potato. Sprinkle with parsley.

Hot Beef on a Tater ———— 4 servings

- 2 cups cubed or shredded cooked roast beef
- 1 can (10 1/4 ounces) beef gravy or 1 1/4 cups homemade beef gravy
- 1 cup frozen peas
- 1/4 cup dry red wine
- 1 medium tomato, seeded and chopped
- 4 Basic Baked Potatoes (page 14), hot

Combine roast beef, gravy, peas, wine, and tomato in 2-quart saucepan; cook on low heat until heated through, stirring occasionally. Open potatoes; fluff insides with fork. Divide and spoon beef mixture over each potato.

Tuna Topper — 2 servings

- 1 tablespoon butter or margarine
- 1 tablespoon all-purpose flour
- 3/4 cup milk, heated
- 1/4 teaspoon seasoned salt
- 1 tablespoon minced parsley
- 3 tablespoons shredded Cheddar or Swiss cheese
- 1 can (3 1/4 ounces) tuna, drained and flaked
- 2 Basic Baked Potatoes (page 14), hot

Melt butter in small saucepan on moderate heat. Stir in flour. While stirring constantly, gradually add milk. Add salt and parsley; cook and stir until thickened and smooth. Stir in cheese and tuna; cook until heated through. Open potatoes; fluff insides with fork. Divide and spoon tuna mixture over each potato.

To prepare this recipe in a microwave oven, use a 2-cup glass measure. Combine flour, 1/2 cup milk, salt, and parsley; blend well. Add butter. Cook on High 1 to 1 1/2 minutes, or until mixture thickens, stirring once during cooking. Stir in cheese and tuna. Cook on High 1 to 1 1/2 minutes, or until cheese is melted and mixture is heated through. Let stand 1 minute on heatproof surface. Serve as directed above.

Zucchini and Tomato Sauce — 4 servings

- 3 tablespoons butter, margarine, or olive oil
- 3 medium zucchini (1 pound), cut into 1/4-inch cubes
- 1/3 cup thinly sliced green onion
- 1/4 teaspoon thyme
- 1 medium tomato, seeded and chopped
- 1/4 teaspoon salt
- Dash pepper
- 4 Basic Baked Potatoes (page 14), hot

Melt butter in medium skillet on medium-high heat. Stir in zucchini, onion, and thyme. Cook, stirring constantly, until vegetables are slightly browned and crisp-tender. Stir in tomato, salt, and pepper; heat through. Open potatoes; fluff insides with fork. Divide and spoon zucchini mixture over each potato.

Chicken à la King ———————— 6 servings

- 1/4 cup butter or margarine
- 1/4 pound fresh mushrooms, sliced
- 1/2 green pepper, seeded and chopped
- 1 can (2 ounces) chopped pimiento, drained
- 3 tablespoons all-purpose flour
- 1/2 teaspoon salt
- 1 cup chicken broth, heated
- 1/2 cup milk, heated
- Dash white pepper
- 1/4 teaspoon turmeric
- 1/2 cup light cream or half-and-half
- 2 egg yolks
- 2 cups cubed cooked chicken
- 1 cup fresh or frozen peas
- 6 Basic Baked Potatoes (page 14), hot

Melt butter in medium saucepan on moderate heat. Add mushrooms, green pepper, and pimiento; sauté until tender. Remove from heat. Stir in flour and salt until smooth. While stirring constantly, gradually add broth and milk. Return to heat. Cook over low heat, stirring constantly, until mixture thickens. Stir in pepper and turmeric. Blend cream and egg yolk in small bowl; stir into thickened mixture. Add chicken and peas; heat through. Open potatoes; fluff insides with fork. Divide and spoon chicken mixture over each potato.

Seafood Thermidor ———————— 6 servings

- 1 tablespoon butter or margarine
- 1/2 cup sliced fresh mushrooms
- 2 cans (10 ounces each) cream of shrimp soup, undiluted
- 1/2 cup milk
- 1 can (7 1/2 ounces) crab meat, drained and picked over
- 2 cans (4 1/2 ounces each) small shrimp, drained
- 1/4 teaspoon dry mustard
- 1/4 teaspoon paprika
- Dash cayenne
- 2 tablespoons dry sherry
- 6 Basic Baked Potatoes (page 14), hot

Melt butter in saucepan. Add mushrooms; stir until heated through. Stir in soup and milk until smooth. Add crab meat, shrimp, mustard, paprika, and cayenne. Heat to a boil, stirring constantly. Remove from heat. Stir in sherry. Open potatoes; fluff insides with fork. Divide and spoon seafood mixture over each potato.

Old-Fashioned Creamed Turkey — 6 servings

- 2 tablespoons butter or margarine
- 1 medium green pepper, seeded and cut into thin strips
- 1/2 pound fresh mushrooms, sliced
- 1 small onion, diced
- 1 can (10 3/4 ounces) cream of mushroom soup, undiluted
- 3 tablespoons chopped, pitted ripe olives
- 1 jar (2 ounces) diced pimiento, drained
- 3 cups cooked turkey, cut into bite-size pieces
- 1/8 teaspoon pepper
- 6 Basic Baked Potatoes (page 14), hot

Melt butter in 3-quart saucepan on moderate heat. Add green pepper, mushrooms, and onion; sauté until tender, stirring occasionally. Stir in soup, olives, pimiento, turkey, 1/2 cup water, and pepper. Simmer 10 minutes. Open potatoes; fluff insides with fork. Divide and spoon turkey mixture over each potato.

Spinach Spud Supreme — 4 servings

- 1 package (10 ounces) frozen chopped spinach, prepared according to package directions
- 6 slices bacon, diced
- 1/4 pound sliced fresh mushrooms
- 2 tablespoons all-purpose flour
- 2 cups chicken broth, heated
- 1/4 teaspoon garlic powder
- 1 cup shredded Swiss cheese
- 4 Basic Baked Potatoes (page 14), hot
- 2 hard-cooked eggs, sliced

Drain spinach; squeeze dry with paper towels; set aside. Fry bacon in large skillet until crisp; remove with slotted spoon; drain on paper towels. Pour off all but 3 tablespoons drippings. Add mushrooms to drippings in skillet; sauté until tender. Remove with slotted spoon. Add flour; blend well. While stirring constantly, gradually add broth and garlic powder; stir until thickened. Stir in spinach, bacon, and mushrooms; heat just to a boil. Remove from heat. Add cheese; stir until cheese is melted. Open potatoes; fluff insides with fork. Divide and spoon spinach mixture over each potato. Top with egg slices.

From the Other Field

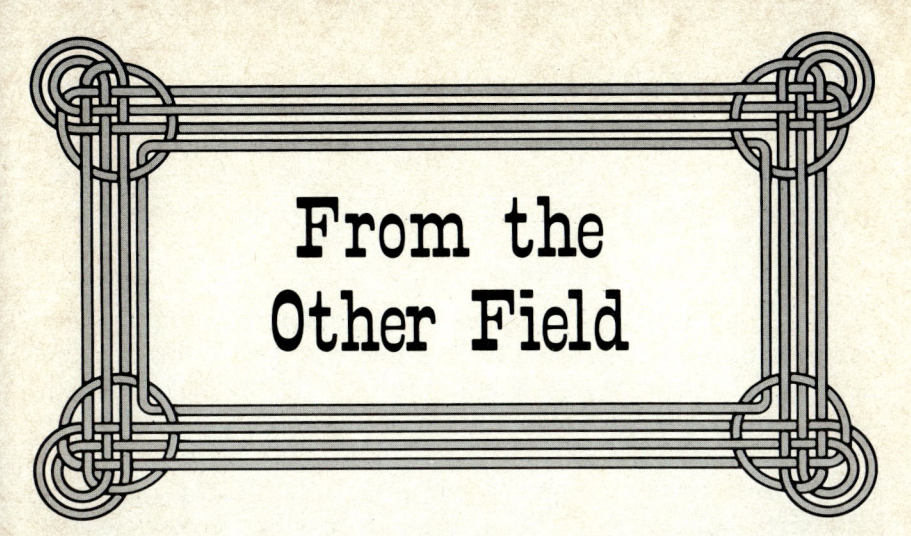

Fields of potatoes are often neighbors of grain fields. In the kitchen, ingenious cooks have married these neighbors in recipes of all kinds. If you were asked, "What kind of baked goods can you make with potatoes?" you might reply, "potato bread" and stop there. But please don't. Why not use these complementary neighbors and bake bread, rolls, muffins, cakes, and doughnuts? Reap the compliments of the harvest!

> In recipes using yeast, we have suggested heating the liquid to 120°F to 130°F. If you do not have a thermometer, scald the milk and cool to lukewarm. To test for lukewarm temperature, drop a little of the liquid on the inside of your wrist. It should feel comfortably warm.

Potato Drop Biscuits — 12 biscuits

1 cup Riced Potatoes (page 22)
3/4 cup all-purpose flour
6 tablespoons milk
1 tablespoon baking powder
1 tablespoon butter or margarine, softened
1 teaspoon salt

Preheat oven to 400°F. Grease a baking sheet; set aside. Combine potatoes, flour, milk, baking powder, butter, and salt in medium bowl; blend thoroughly with fork. Divide and spoon mixture onto prepared baking sheet in 12 equal portions. Bake 15 to 20 minutes, or until bottoms of biscuits are brown and tops are beginning to brown. Serve warm or cool.

Potato Baking Powder Biscuits ——————— 1 dozen

- 2 cups all-purpose flour
- 1 cup Mashed Potatoes (page 13)
- 1 tablespoon baking powder
- 1 teaspoon salt
- 1/4 cup vegetable shortening
- 3 tablespoons milk

Preheat oven to 450°F. Combine flour, potatoes, baking powder, salt, and shortening in large bowl; blend with pastry blender until mixture is consistency of coarse crumbs. Stir in milk just until mixture is moistened. Turn dough out onto lightly floured surface. Knead 2 to 3 minutes. Roll dough out to 1/2-inch thickness. Use a 2-inch round biscuit cutter to cut about 12 biscuits. Place on ungreased baking sheet. Bake 12 to 15 minutes, or until golden brown. Remove from baking sheet to wire rack to cool slightly before serving.

Crunchy Bran Muffins ——————— 18 muffins

- 1 1/2 cups bran cereal
- 1 1/4 cups milk
- 1 1/4 cups all-purpose flour
- 1 cup finely crushed Potato Chips (page 18), divided
- 1/2 cup sugar
- 1/2 cup raisins
- 1/3 cup vegetable oil
- 1 egg
- 3 teaspoons baking powder
- 1/2 teaspoon salt
- 3 tablespoons chopped nuts

Preheat oven to 400°F. Combine cereal and milk in large bowl; let stand 5 minutes. Stir in flour, half of the crushed chips, sugar, raisins, oil, egg, baking powder, and salt. Mix just until combined. Divide and spoon into 18 paper-lined muffin cups. Lightly toss remaining chips and nuts in small bowl. Sprinkle on top of each muffin. Bake 15 to 20 minutes. Serve warm.

Potato Ice Box Rolls — 2 1/2 to 3 dozen

- 1 cup milk
- 1/2 cup shortening
- 6 to 7 cups all-purpose flour, divided
- 1 cup Mashed Potatoes (page 13), at room temperature
- 2 packages (1/4 ounce each) active dry yeast
- 2 tablespoons sugar
- 1 teaspoon salt
- 2 eggs

Heat milk, 1/2 cup water, and shortening in small saucepan to 120°F to 130°F. Combine 1 cup flour, potatoes, yeast, sugar, salt, and warm milk mixture in large bowl. Beat with electric mixer on low until thoroughly blended. Beat on high for 2 minutes. Add eggs and 1/2 cup flour; beat 2 minutes. Stir in enough remaining flour to make a stiff dough. Turn dough out onto lightly floured surface. Knead 10 minutes, or until smooth and elastic. Place in lightly greased bowl and turn to coat entire surface. Cover with oiled waxed paper, then with aluminum foil. Refrigerate at least 4 hours or up to 24 hours. Grease a baking sheet. Shape dough as desired. Place on prepared baking sheet. Let rise in warm place, free from draft, until almost double in bulk, about 1 hour. Preheat oven to 375°F. Bake 20 to 25 minutes, or until golden brown. Remove from baking sheet to wire racks; cool slightly before serving.

Potato Waffles — 6 servings

- 1 1/2 cups milk
- 2 eggs
- 1 tablespoon vegetable oil
- 1 cup all-purpose flour
- 1/3 cup instant potato flakes
- 2 teaspoons sugar
- 2 teaspoons baking powder
- 1/2 teaspoon salt

Combine milk, eggs, and oil in large bowl; beat with electric mixer until thoroughly blended. Add remaining ingredients; mix well. Cook waffles on electric waffle iron, according to manufacturer's directions, until golden brown. Serve hot with butter and maple syrup.

Wisconsin Spice Cake ———————— 12 servings

- 1 1/2 cups sugar
- 3/4 cup vegetable shortening
- 1 cup Mashed Potatoes (page 13), at room temperature
- 3 eggs, slightly beaten
- 2 cups all-purpose flour
- 1/2 teaspoon cinnamon
- 1/2 teaspoon salt
- 1/2 teaspoon nutmeg
- 1 teaspoon baking powder
- 1 cup milk
- 3/4 cup raisins
- Caramel Frosting (below)

Preheat oven to 350°F. Grease and flour a 9 × 13-inch pan; set aside. Cream sugar and shortening in large bowl until fluffy. Add potatoes and eggs; blend well. Combine flour, cinnamon, salt, nutmeg, and baking powder in small bowl; mix lightly. Alternately beat dry ingredients and milk into creamed mixture until well blended. Stir in raisins. Pour into prepared pan. Bake 45 to 55 minutes, or until toothpick inserted in center comes out clean. Cool completely before frosting with Caramel Frosting.

For a festive occasion, prepare this cake in a bundt-type pan.

Caramel Frosting

- 1/4 cup butter or margarine
- 1 cup firmly packed light brown sugar
- 3 1/2 tablespoons milk
- 2 cups confectioners sugar

Melt butter and brown sugar in small saucepan on low heat. Cook about 2 minutes, stirring constantly. Add milk; bring to a full boil on medium-high heat, stirring constantly. Remove from heat. Cool slightly. Beat in sugar with electric mixer until consistency is easily spreadable.   2 1/2 cups

Wisconsin Spice Cake, Potato Kolache (page 102)

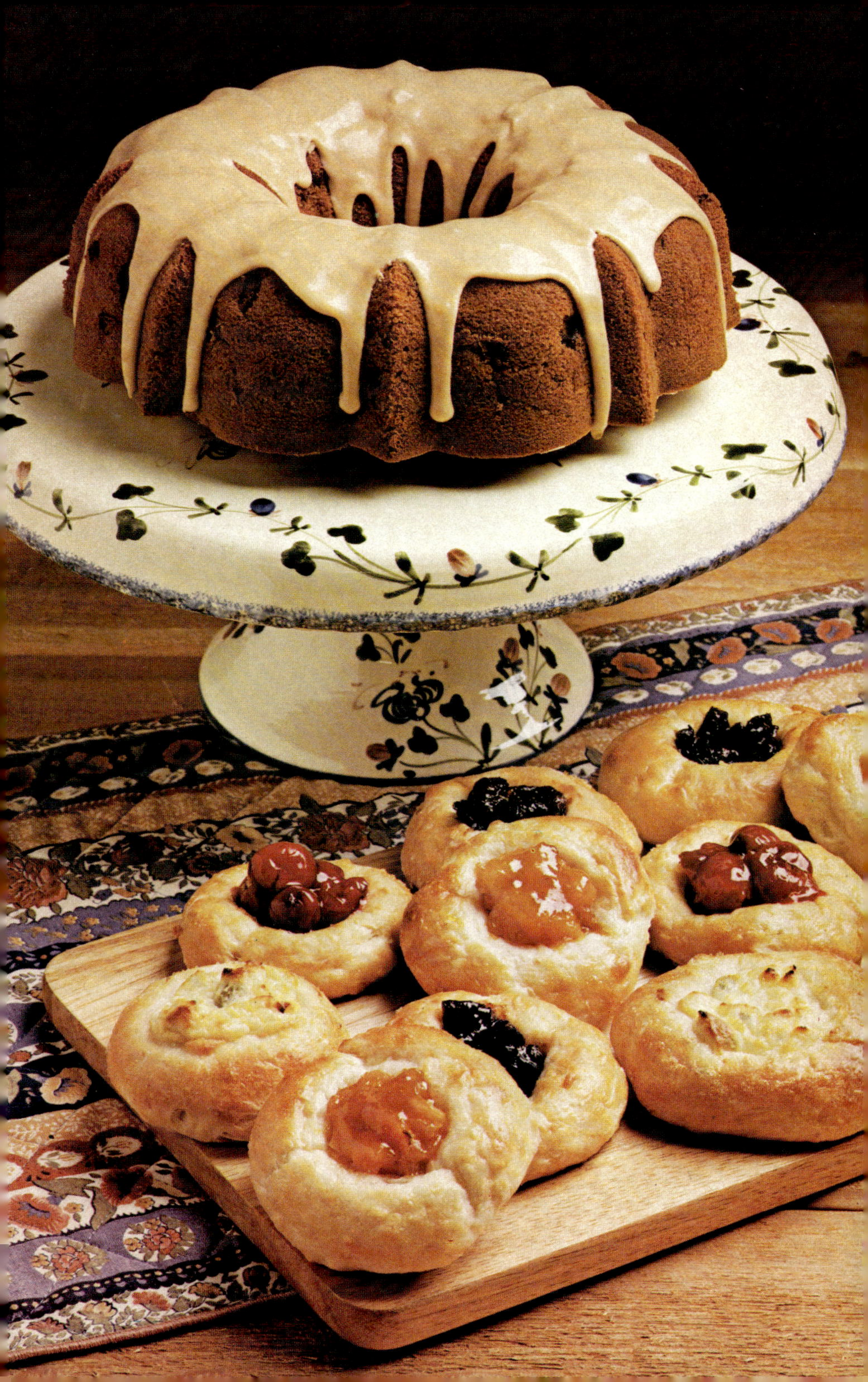

Potato Kolache —————————————— 6 dozen

1 medium potato, washed and peeled	2 packages (1/4 ounce each) active dry yeast
1 cup butter or margarine	1 can (13 ounces) evaporated milk, undiluted
5 1/2 to 6 1/2 cups all-purpose flour, divided	
1 teaspoon salt	2 eggs, slightly beaten
1/2 cup sugar	

Boil potato in water until tender; drain; reserve potato water. Add enough water to potato water to equal 1 1/2 cups. Mash potato until smooth; set aside. Combine 4 cups flour, salt, sugar, and yeast in large bowl. Combine potatoes, potato water, milk, and butter in saucepan. Heat to 120°F to 130°F. Remove from heat. Stir into flour mixture. Add eggs; blend thoroughly. Stir in enough remaining flour to make a soft dough. Cover. Let rise in warm place, free from draft, until almost double in bulk, about 1 hour. Grease a baking sheet; set aside. Punch dough down. Pinch off walnut-size pieces of dough; roll each into a ball. Place about 1 inch apart on prepared baking sheet. Make a depression in the center of each ball, pushing dough toward edge, leaving a 1/4-inch rim around edge. Fill centers with approximately 2 teaspoons filling. (Use your favorite jam, canned fillings, or one of the fillings below.) Let rise in warm place, free from draft, until almost double in bulk, about 20 minutes. Preheat oven to 375°F. Bake 15 to 20 minutes, or until light golden brown. Cool on wire rack.

Prune Filling

1/2 pound dried pitted prunes, cut up	2 tablespoons sugar
	1 tablespoon lemon juice

Combine all ingredients in saucepan with 1 cup water. Cook on low heat, stirring occasionally, 10 minutes, or until thickened.

Cheese Filling

2 egg yolks	1 tablespoon butter
1 tablespoon honey	1 cup ricotta cheese

Combine all ingredients in saucepan. Cook on low heat, stirring occasionally, 10 minutes, or until thickened.

Apricot Filling

1/2 pound dried pitted apricots, chopped

1/4 cup sugar

Combine ingredients in saucepan with 1 1/4 cups water. Bring to a boil. Simmer, stirring occasionally, 15 minutes, or until thickened.

Potato Cinnamon Rolls — 18 rolls

- 1 cup Mashed Potatoes (page 13), at room temperature; reserve 1 cup potato water
- 5 1/2 to 6 1/2 cups all-purpose flour, divided
- 1/2 cup sugar
- 1/2 cup vegetable shortening, melted
- 1 teaspoon salt
- 2 packages (1/4 ounce each) active dry yeast
- 2 eggs
- 2 tablespoons butter, melted
- 1/4 cup sugar
- 1 1/2 teaspoons cinnamon

Heat reserved potato water in small saucepan to 120°F to 130°F. Combine 1 cup flour, potatoes, potato water, sugar, shortening, salt, and yeast in large bowl; beat with electric mixer 2 minutes. Add eggs and 1/2 cup flour; beat 2 minutes. Stir in enough remaining flour to make a stiff dough. Turn dough out onto lightly floured surface. Knead 8 to 10 minutes, or until smooth and elastic. Place in lightly greased bowl and turn to coat entire surface. Cover and let rise in warm place, free from draft, until almost double in bulk, about 1 hour. Divide dough in half. Shape each half into a ball; cover 1 ball; set aside. Roll out other ball on lightly floured surface into a 9 × 14 × 1/2-inch rectangle. Brush with half of the melted butter. Combine sugar and cinnamon in small dish. Sprinkle dough with half of the sugar-cinnamon mixture. Beginning at narrow end, roll up dough. Cut into 9 equal slices. Grease an 8-inch square pan. Place slices, cut-side up, in prepared pan. Repeat with remaining dough. Cover and let rise in warm place, free from draft, until almost double in bulk, about 1 hour. Preheat oven to 375°F. Bake 20 to 25 minutes, or until golden brown.

Potato Cherry Nut Loaf ———————— 1 loaf

- 3/4 cup milk
- 2 1/2 cups all-purpose flour, divided
- 1 cup Mashed Potatoes (page 13), room temperature
- 2 packages (1/4 ounce each) active dry yeast
- 1/4 cup sugar
- 2 tablespoons vegetable shortening
- 1 teaspoon salt
- 1/2 cup chopped candied cherries
- 1/2 cup raisins
- 1/4 cup chopped nuts

Grease a 9 × 5-inch loaf pan; set aside. Heat milk and 1/2 cup water in small saucepan to 120°F to 130°F. Combine 1 cup flour, potatoes, yeast, warm milk and water, sugar, shortening, and salt in large bowl; beat with electric mixer until thoroughly blended. Beat on high 2 minutes. Stir in remaining flour, cherries, raisins, and nuts. Cover and let rise in warm place, free from draft, until almost double in bulk, about 1 hour. Stir dough down. Pour into prepared pan. Cover and let rise in warm place, free from draft, 30 minutes. Preheat oven to 375°F. Bake 30 to 40 minutes, or until toothpick inserted in center comes out clean. Remove from pan to cool on wire rack.

Mashed Potato Spice Cake ———————— 12 servings

- 2 cups sugar
- 1 cup butter or margarine, softened
- 4 eggs, separated
- 1 cup Mashed Potatoes (page 13), at room temperature
- 1 cup chopped walnuts
- 1 teaspoon cinnamon
- 1 teaspoon cloves
- 1 teaspoon nutmeg
- 2 1/2 cups all-purpose flour
- 1/2 cup milk
- 2 teaspoons baking powder

Preheat oven to 350°F. Grease and flour a 9 × 13-inch pan; set aside. Cream sugar and butter in large bowl with electric mixer until fluffy. Add egg yolks, potatoes, walnuts, cinnamon, cloves, and nutmeg; beat until smooth. Stir in flour, milk, and baking powder. Beat egg whites in small bowl with electric mixer until stiff. Carefully fold whites into batter. Pour into prepared pan. Bake 45 minutes, or until toothpick inserted in center comes out clean. Dust with confectioners sugar, or serve topped with your favorite ice cream.

Quick Potato Coffee Cake ———————— 10 to 12 servings

- 1 1/2 cups all-purpose flour
- 1 egg, slightly beaten
- 3/4 cup sugar
- 3/4 cup milk
- 1/2 cup Mashed Potatoes (page 13), at room temperature
- 1/2 cup butter or margarine, softened
- 2 teaspoons baking powder
- 1 teaspoon vanilla
- 1/2 teaspoon salt
- 1/4 cup firmly packed light brown sugar
- 2 tablespoons sugar
- 1 teaspoon cinnamon

Preheat oven to 350°F. Grease a 9 × 13-inch baking pan; set aside. Combine flour, eggs, sugar, milk, potatoes, butter, baking powder, vanilla, and salt in large bowl; beat with electric mixer until thoroughly blended. Pour into prepared pan; spreading evenly. Combine brown sugar, sugar, and cinnamon in small bowl; stir with fork to blend. Sprinkle over batter. Bake 20 to 25 minutes, or until coffee cake is golden brown. Cool in pan for 20 minutes before cutting into squares.

Applesauce Potato Bread ———————— 1 loaf

- 1 cup sugar
- 1 egg
- 3 tablespoons vegetable oil
- 1 cup Mashed Potatoes (page 13), at room temperature
- 1 3/4 cups all-purpose flour
- 1/2 teaspoon baking soda
- 2 teaspoons baking powder
- 1/2 teaspoon salt
- 1/2 teaspoon cinnamon
- 1/4 teaspoon nutmeg
- 1 cup applesauce
- 1/2 cup chopped nuts
- 1/3 cup raisins

Preheat oven to 350°F. Grease a 9 × 5-inch loaf pan; set aside. Combine sugar, egg, and oil in large bowl; beat with electric mixer until thoroughly blended. Add potatoes; blend well. Combine flour, baking soda, baking powder, salt, cinnamon, and nutmeg in separate bowl. Alternately add dry ingredients and applesauce to potato mixture, blending well after each addition. Stir in nuts and raisins. Pour into prepared pan. Bake 1 hour and 15 minutes, or until toothpick inserted in center comes out clean. Remove from oven to wire rack. Cool completely before slicing.

Slim Chocolate Cake ———— 16 servings

- 1/2 cup sugar
- 1/2 cup firmly packed light brown sugar
- 1/2 cup granulated sugar substitute
- 1/3 cup diet margarine, softened
- 4 eggs
- 2 cups cake flour
- 1 cup Mashed Potatoes (page 13), at room temperature
- 1/2 cup skim milk
- 6 tablespoons cocoa
- 1 tablespoon baking powder
- 1 teaspoon vanilla
- 1/2 teaspoon salt
- 1/2 teaspoon cinnamon
- Chocolate Frosting (page 107)

Preheat oven to 350°F. Grease and flour two 8-inch round cake pans; set aside. Cream sugar, brown sugar, sugar substitute, and margarine in large bowl with electric mixer until fluffy. Add eggs, 1 at a time, beating well after each addition. Stir in remaining ingredients; beat until smooth. Pour into prepared pans. Bake 45 to 50 minutes, or until toothpick inserted in center comes out clean. Cool cakes in pans 15 minutes; invert onto wire rack to cool completely. Frost with Chocolate Frosting.

Classic Potato Cake ———— 12 to 14 servings

- 3 egg whites
- 2 cups sugar
- 1/2 cup butter or margarine, softened
- 1 cup Mashed Potatoes (page 13), warm
- 1 teaspoon vanilla
- 1 teaspoon cocoa
- 2 cups all-purpose flour
- 2 teaspoons baking powder
- 1/4 teaspoon baking soda
- 1/2 cup milk
- 3/4 cup chopped pecans
- Chocolate Frosting (page 107)

Preheat oven to 350°F. Grease and flour two 8-inch round cake pans; set aside. Beat egg whites in small bowl with electric mixer until stiff peaks form; set aside. Cream sugar and butter in large bowl with electric mixer until fluffy. Add potatoes, vanilla, and cocoa; beat until blended. Stir in flour, baking powder, and baking soda. Stir in milk and nuts. Carefully fold in egg whites until no white remains. Divide and pour into prepared pans. Bake 35 to 40 minutes, or until toothpick inserted in center comes out clean. Cool completely in pan on wire rack. Frost with Chocolate Frosting.

Chocolate Frosting

- 2 cups confectioners sugar
- 2 squares (2 ounces each) semisweet chocolate, melted
- 1/3 cup butter or margarine, melted
- 1 1/2 teaspoons vanilla
- 4 to 6 tablespoons hot water, divided

Combine sugar, chocolate, butter, vanilla, and 3 tablespoons water in small bowl. Beat with electric mixer, adding 1 tablespoon water at a time, until spreading consistency.   1 1/2 cups

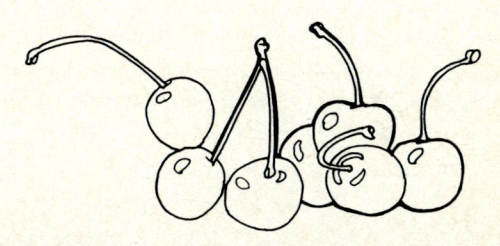

Cherry Cheesecake ———————— 8 servings

- 2 cups crushed Potato Chips (page 18)
- 1/4 cup all-purpose flour
- 1/4 cup confectioners sugar
- 1 tablespoon vegetable oil
- 3 eggs
- 3 packages (3 ounces each) cream cheese, softened
- 1 cup sugar
- 2 teaspoons grated lemon peel
- 1/2 teaspoon vanilla
- 1 can (16 ounces) pitted tart red cherries, drained; reserve liquid
- 3/4 cup sugar
- 2 tablespoons cornstarch

Preheat oven to 350°F. Combine chips, flour confectioners sugar, and oil in medium bowl; blend well. Press mixture into bottom of 9-inch springform pan. Bake 10 minutes. Combine eggs, cream cheese, sugar, lemon peel, and vanilla in large bowl; beat with electric mixer until smooth. Pour over crust; spread evenly to edge. Reduce oven temperature to 300°F. Bake 1 hour, or until filling is set. Cool in pan on wire rack 1 hour. Pour reserved cherry liquid into small saucepan. Add sugar and cornstarch; stir to dissolve cornstarch. Cook on high heat until mixture comes to a rolling boil, stirring constantly. Cook until clear and thickened, stirring constantly. Stir in cherries. Spoon cherry mixture evenly over cheesecake. Refrigerate at least 3 hours before serving.

Raised Potato Doughnuts ——————— 3 dozen

- 1 1/2 cups Riced Potatoes (page 22), at room temperature; reserve 1 3/4 cups potato water
- 5 to 6 cups all-purpose flour, divided
- 3/4 cup vegetable shortening
- 1/2 cup sugar
- 2 packages (1/4 ounce each) active dry yeast
- 1 teaspoon salt
- 1/2 teaspoon cinnamon
- 1/4 teaspoon nutmeg
- 2 eggs
- Peanut or corn oil for deep-fat frying
- Creamy Frosting (below)

Heat reserved potato water in small saucepan to 120°F to 130°F. Combine 1 cup flour, potatoes, warm potato water, shortening, sugar, yeast, salt, cinnamon, and nutmeg in large bowl. Beat with electric mixer on high 2 minutes. Add 1 cup flour and eggs; beat on high 2 minutes. Stir in enough remaining flour to make a stiff dough. Turn out onto lightly floured surface. Knead 8 to 10 minutes, or until smooth and elastic. Place dough in lightly greased bowl and turn to coat entire surface. Cover and let rise in warm place, free from draft, until almost double in bulk, about 1 hour. Turn dough out onto lightly floured surface; roll out to 1/2-inch thickness. Use a floured 2 1/2-inch doughnut cutter to cut doughnuts. Place doughnuts on lightly floured baking sheets. Cover with oiled waxed paper. Let rise in warm place, free from draft, 20 minutes. Heat 4 inches oil in large saucepan to 375°F. Drop 3 or 4 doughnuts into oil. Fry 2 to 3 minutes on each side, or until golden brown. Lift out with slotted spoon; drain on paper towels. Repeat for remaining doughnuts. Frost with Creamy Frosting.

Creamy Frosting

- 2 cups confectioners sugar
- 1/3 cup butter or margarine
- 1 1/2 teaspoons vanilla
- 4 to 6 tablespoons hot water, divided

Combine sugar, butter, vanilla, and 3 tablespoons water in small bowl. Beat with electric mixer, adding 1 tablespoon water at a time, until spreading consistency. Spread on warm doughnuts.

Jelly-Filled Drop Doughnuts ——— 1 dozen

- 4 cups all-purpose flour, divided
- 3 eggs
- 1 1/3 cups sugar
- 1 cup Mashed Potatoes (page 13), at room temperature
- 1/2 cup milk
- 2 tablespoons vegetable shortening, melted
- 2 tablespoons baking powder
- 2 teaspoons nutmeg
- 1 teaspoon salt
- Peanut or corn oil for deep-fat frying
- 1 cup raspberry jelly

Combine 2 cups flour, eggs, sugar, potatoes, milk, shortening, baking powder, nutmeg, and salt in large bowl. Beat with electric mixer until smooth. Stir in remaining flour. Cover bowl with plastic wrap. Chill 3 hours. Heat about 4 inches oil in large saucepan to 375°F. Drop dough into oil by large, rounded tablespoonfuls. Deep-fat fry 10 to 12 minutes, or until golden brown, turning doughnuts with slotted spoon to cook evenly. Drain on paper towels. Cut small hole in one side of each doughnut with sharp knife. Spoon in about 1 tablespoon jelly; place on wire rack. Let stand until cool.

Aunt Gypsy's Doughnuts ——— 2 dozen

- 2 tablespoons vegetable oil
- 1 egg
- 1/2 cup milk
- 2 3/4 cups all-purpose flour
- 2 1/2 teaspoons baking powder
- 1 teaspoon salt
- 1 cup sugar
- 1 teaspoon nutmeg
- 1/2 teaspoon cinnamon
- 1 cup Riced Potatoes (page 22), at room temperature
- Peanut or corn oil for deep-fat frying

Combine oil, egg, and milk in large bowl; blend well. Combine flour, baking powder, salt, sugar, nutmeg, and cinnamon in separate bowl; mix lightly. Gradually add dry ingredients to milk mixture. Add potatoes; blend thoroughly. Roll out on lightly floured surface to 1/2-inch thickness. (Add enough additional flour to make dough manageable.) Use a floured 3-inch doughnut cutter to cut about 2 dozen doughnuts. Heat oil to 365°F. Carefully add doughnuts to hot oil. Fry 3 to 5 minutes, or until cooked through and golden brown. Drain on paper towels. Dip in confectioners sugar, granulated sugar, or a mixture of cinnamon and granulated sugar.

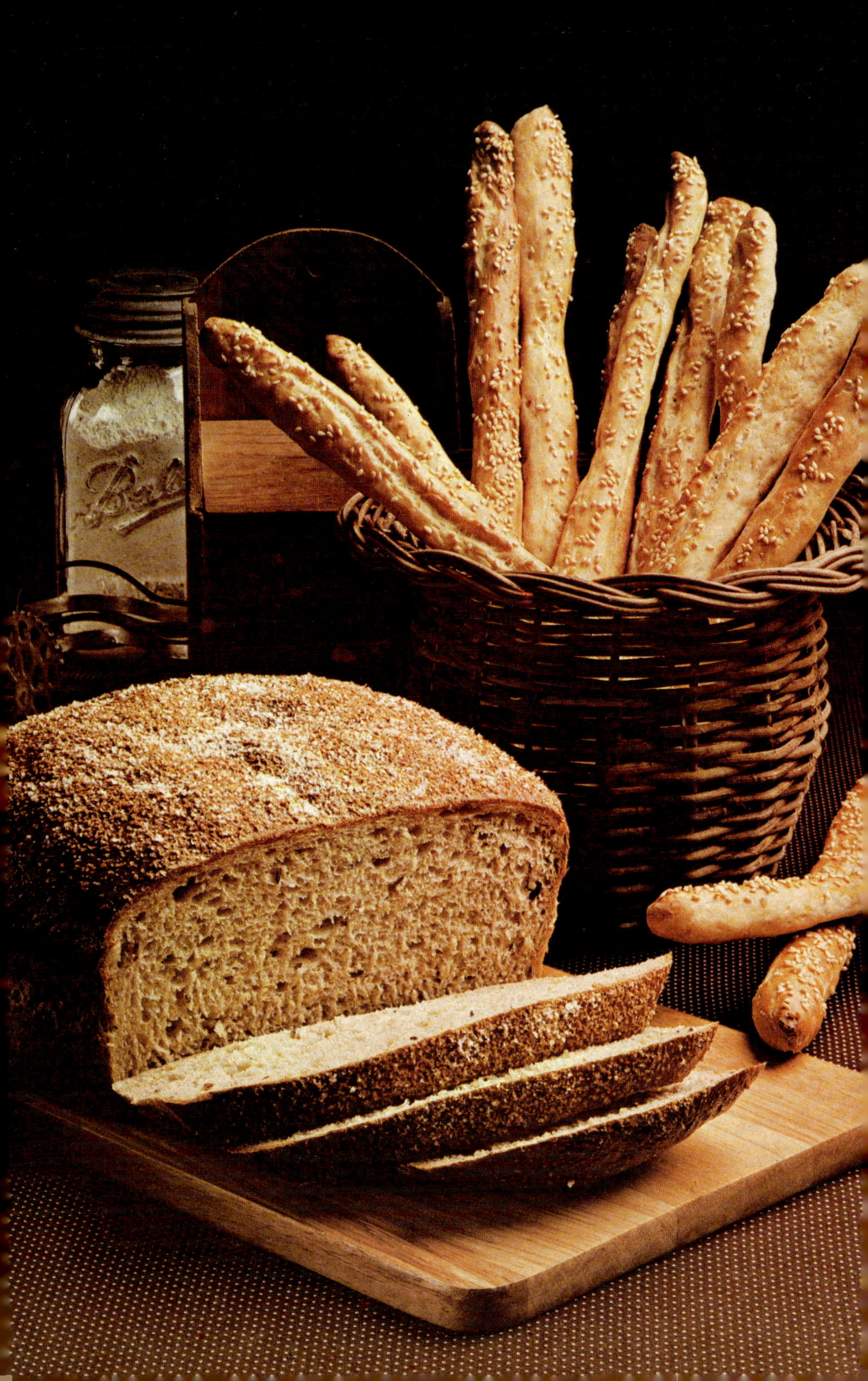

Potato Bread Sticks — 20 to 24 sticks

- 1 medium potato, washed, cooked, peeled, and mashed; reserve 2/3 cup potato water
- 3 1/2 to 4 cups all-purpose flour, divided
- 1 package (1/4 ounce) active dry yeast
- 1/4 cup vegetable oil
- 1 teaspoon sugar
- 1 teaspoon salt
- 1 egg white
- Toasted sesame seed

Grease a baking sheet; set aside. Heat reserved potato water in small saucepan to 120°F to 130°F. Combine potato, warm potato water, 1 1/2 cups flour, yeast, oil, sugar, and salt in large bowl. Beat with electric mixer on high 2 minutes. Stir in remaining flour. Divide into 20 to 24 equal parts. Roll each part into a 1/2 to 3/4-inch rope. Place, 1 inch apart, on prepared baking sheet. Cover with oiled waxed paper. Let rest 20 minutes. Preheat oven to 350°F. Beat egg white and 1 tablespoon water with fork in small bowl. Brush over bread sticks. Sprinkle with sesame seed. Bake 25 to 30 minutes, or until golden brown. Cool before serving.

Potato Roll-Ups — 9 servings

- 3 eggs
- 3 medium potatoes, washed, peeled, and grated
- 1 medium onion, peeled and grated
- 1/3 cup matzo meal
- 1/4 cup all-purpose flour
- 1/4 cup lemon juice
- 1/4 teaspoon salt
- 1/8 teaspoon pepper
- Butter or margarine

Combine eggs, potatoes, onion, matzo meal, flour, juice, salt, and pepper in bowl of food processor fitted with steel blade or in large mixing bowl. Thoroughly butter small skillet, sauté, or crêpe pan; heat until hot. Pour in enough batter to cover bottom, about 1/3 cup; tilt pan to spread batter evenly. Turn crêpe when bottom is browned; brown other side. Remove from pan; place on plate. Cover with aluminum foil to keep warm. Repeat with remaining batter, adding more butter as necessary. Serve warm, filled with applesauce or your choice of fruit.

Potato Bread Sticks, Country Rye Bread (page 112)

Country Rye Bread — 1 loaf

- 1 cup Mashed Potatoes (page 13), at room temperature; reserve 1 1/2 cups potato water
- 2 1/2 to 3 cups all-purpose flour, divided
- 1 1/2 cups rye flour
- 1 package (1/4 ounce) active dry yeast
- 1 tablespoon sugar
- 1 tablespoon butter or margarine
- 2 teaspoons caraway seed
- 1 teaspoon salt
- 1 egg, slightly beaten
- 2 tablespoons coarse salt

Heat reserved potato water in small saucepan to 120°F to 130°F. Combine 1 cup all-purpose flour, rye flour, potatoes, warm potato water, yeast, sugar, butter, caraway seed, and salt in large bowl. Beat with electric mixer on high 2 minutes. Stir in remaining flour. Turn dough out onto lightly floured surface. Knead 10 minutes, or until dough is smooth and elastic. Place in lightly greased bowl; turn to coat entire surface. Cover and let rise in warm place, free from draft, until almost double in bulk, about 1 hour. Grease an 8-inch round cake pan; set aside. Punch dough down. Shape into a smooth, round ball. Place in prepared pan. Cover. Let rise in warm place, free from draft, until almost double in bulk, about 1 hour. Preheat oven to 375°F. Brush surface with beaten egg. Sprinkle with coarse salt. Bake 40 to 50 minutes, or until loaf sounds hollow when lightly tapped. Remove from pan. Cool on wire rack.

Cinnamon Twist Coffee Cake — 12 servings

- 1/2 cup milk
- 4 tablespoons butter or margarine, divided
- 3 to 3 1/2 cups all-purpose flour, divided
- 2/3 cup sugar
- 1/2 cup Mashed Potatoes (page 13), at room temperature
- 1 package (1/4 ounce) active dry yeast
- 3/4 teaspoon salt
- 1 egg
- 1/2 cup raisins
- 1 teaspoon cinnamon
- 2 teaspoons sugar, divided

Grease an 8-inch round pan; set aside. Heat milk, 1/3 cup water, and 2 tablespoons butter in small saucepan to 120°F to 130°F; set aside. Combine 1 cup flour, 2/3 cup sugar, potatoes, yeast, and salt in large mixing bowl. Gradually beat in warm milk mixture with electric mixer. Beat on high speed 2 minutes. Add egg and 1/2 cup flour; beat 2 minutes. Stir in raisins and remaining flour to make a stiff dough. Turn dough out onto lightly floured surface. Knead 8 to 10 minutes, or until smooth and elastic. Cover with oiled waxed paper; let rest 20 minutes. Roll dough out into 12-inch square. Melt remaining 2 tablespoons butter; brush part of butter over surface of dough. Combine cinnamon and 1 teaspoon sugar; sprinkle half of the cinnamon-sugar mixture over dough. Fold one-third of dough over center third. Sprinkle with remaining cinnamon-sugar mixture. Fold remaining third of dough over top. Cut lengthwise into 3 equal pieces. Grasp both ends of one of the strips; twist tightly in opposite directions; seal ends. Repeat with remaining strips. place 1 strip around outside edge of prepared pan. Add remaining strips to center of pan. Brush on remaining butter. Sprinkle on remaining 1 teaspoon sugar. Cover with oiled waxed paper; seal with plastic wrap. Refrigerate at least 2 hours or up to 24 hours. To bake, preheat oven to 375°F. Remove pan from refrigerator. Remove cover. Let stand at room temperature 10 minutes. Bake 30 minutes, or until golden brown. Serve warm.

Orange Potato Bread — 1 loaf

- 1 egg
- 1 tablespoon vegetable oil
- 1 teaspoon grated orange peel
- 1/2 teaspoon vanilla
- 3/4 cup Riced Potatoes (page 22)
- 2 3/4 cups all-purpose flour
- 1 cup sugar
- 2 1/2 teaspoons baking powder
- 1 teaspoon salt
- 1 teaspoon baking soda
- 1 1/4 cups orange juice
- 1/2 cup chopped nuts

Preheat oven to 350°F. Grease a 9×5-inch loaf pan; set aside. Combine egg, oil, orange peel, and vanilla in large bowl; beat with electric mixer until thoroughly blended. Add potatoes; blend well. Combine flour, sugar, baking powder, salt, and baking soda in separate bowl. Alternately add dry ingredients and orange juice to potato mixture, blending thoroughly after each addition. Stir in nuts. Pour into prepared pan. Bake 55 to 60 minutes, or until toothpick inserted in center comes out clean. Remove from pan to cool on wire rack.

Potato Bread ———————————————————— 1 loaf

- 1 package (1/4 ounce) active dry yeast
- 1/4 cup warm water (105°F to 115°F)
- 2 cups Mashed Potatoes (page 13), room temperature
- 1 cup milk
- 2 tablespoons butter or margarine, melted
- 2 tablespoons sugar
- 1/2 teaspoon salt
- 4 to 4 1/2 cups all-purpose flour, divided

Dissolve yeast in water in measuring cup. Heat milk in small saucepan to 120°F to 130°F. Combine dissolved yeast, potatoes, warm milk, butter, sugar, salt, and 1 cup flour in large bowl. Mix until smooth. Stir in enough remaining flour to make a stiff dough. Turn dough out onto lightly floured surface. Knead 8 to 10 minutes, or until smooth and elastic. Place in lightly greased bowl; turn to coat entire surface. Cover and let rise in warm place, free from draft, until almost double in bulk, about 1 hour. Punch dough down. Grease a 9×5-inch loaf pan; set aside. Turn dough out onto lightly floured surface; shape into a loaf. Place in prepared pan. Cover and let rise in warm place, free from draft, until almost double in bulk, about 45 minutes. Preheat oven to 375°F. Bake 40 to 45 minutes, or until bread sounds hollow when lightly tapped. Remove from pan. Cool on wire rack.

Honey Whole Wheat Bread ——————— 2 loaves

- 5 1/2 to 6 cups all-purpose flour, divided
- 1 1/2 cups whole-wheat flour
- 1 1/2 cups warm water (120°F to 130°F)
- 1 cup Mashed Potatoes (page 13), at room temperature
- 1/3 cup honey
- 1/4 cup vegetable shortening
- 2 packages (1/4 ounce each) active dry yeast
- 1 1/2 teaspoons salt

Grease two 9×5-inch loaf pans; set aside. Combine 1 cup all-purpose flour, whole-wheat flour, water, potatoes, honey, shortening, yeast, and salt in large bowl. Beat with electric mixer on high 2 minutes. Gradually stir in remaining flour. Turn dough out onto lightly floured surface. Knead 10 minutes, or until smooth and elastic. Place in lightly greased bowl and turn to coat entire surface.

Cover and let rise in warm place, free from draft, until almost double in bulk, about 1 hour. Punch dough down. Divide in half. Shape each half into a loaf. Place loaves in prepared pans. Cover. Let rise in warm place, free from draft, until almost double in bulk, about 1 hour. Preheat oven to 375°F. Bake for 30 to 35 minutes, or until loaves sound hollow when lightly tapped. Remove from pans. Cool on wire rack.

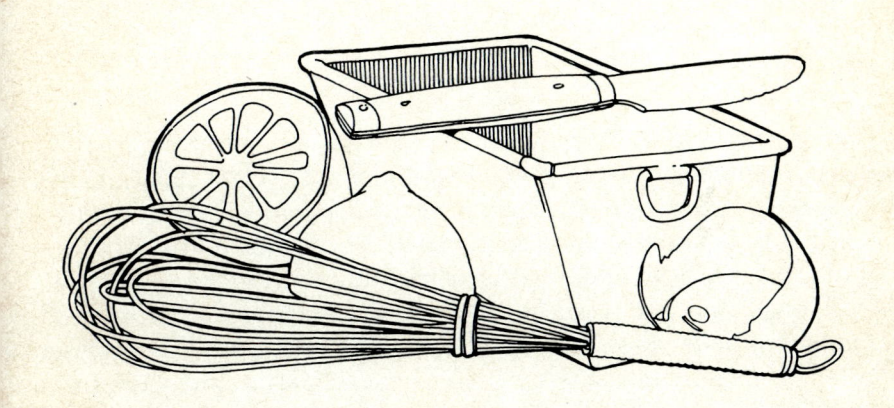

Lemon Potato Bread ——————————— 1 loaf

- 1 1/2 cups sugar, divided
- 6 tablespoons butter or margarine, softened
- 2 eggs
- 1 cup all-purpose flour
- 1 cup Mashed Potatoes (page 13), at room temperature
- 1 1/2 teaspoons baking powder
- 1 teaspoon grated lemon peel
- 1/2 teaspoon salt
- 1/2 cup fresh lemon juice, divided

Preheat oven to 350°F. Grease a 9×5-inch loaf pan; set aside. Cream 1 cup sugar and butter in large bowl with electric mixer until light and fluffy. Add eggs, one at a time, beating after each addition. Add flour, potatoes, baking powder, lemon peel, salt, and 1/4 cup lemon juice; mix well. Pour into prepared pan. Bake 45 to 60 minutes, or until toothpick inserted in center comes out clean. While loaf is baking, heat remaining 1/4 cup lemon juice and 1/2 cup sugar in small saucepan until sugar dissolves; keep warm. Remove loaf from oven. Cool 15 minutes in pan. Spoon syrup over loaf. Cool 30 minutes before removing from pan.

Potato Honey Dips ———————————— 2 dozen

- 2/3 cup honey
- 3 to 3 1/2 cups all-purpose flour, divided
- 1 cup Mashed Potatoes (page 13), at room temperature
- 3 tablespoons sugar
- 1 teaspoon salt
- 1 package (1/4 ounce) active dry yeast
- 1 cup milk
- 2 tablespoons butter or margarine, room temperature
- 2 eggs
- Peanut or corn oil for deep-fat frying

Heat honey and 1/3 cup water in small saucepan until hot; stir to blend. Refrigerate while preparing doughnuts. Heat milk and 1/4 cup water in separate small saucepan to 120°F to 130°F. Combine 1 cup flour, potatoes, sugar, salt, yeast, warm milk and water, and butter in large bowl. Beat with electric mixer on medium 2 minutes. Add eggs and 1/2 cup flour. Beat 2 minutes. Stir in enough remaining flour to make a stiff dough. Cover with oiled waxed paper. Let rise in warm place, free from draft, until almost double in bulk, about 1 hour. Stir dough down. Heat about 4 inches oil in large saucepan to 375°F. Drop dough into oil by rounded tablespoonfuls. Deep-fat fry 5 to 6 minutes, or until golden brown, turning doughnuts with slotted spoon to cook evenly. Drain on paper towels. Immerse doughnuts in chilled honey mixture; drain on wire rack over paper towels.

Not Only From Ireland

The vegetable that conquered the world has had more recipes developed for it than any other vegetable. It's difficult to name a country that doesn't have a favorite potato dish. In this "travel guide," we've included a cross-section of some of the finest from around the world. Cornish Pasty, Vichyssoise, Flemish Pork - no matter what the language or nationality, enjoyment is the common denominator.

Milan Potato Mold — 6 to 8 servings

- 2 tablespoons fine dry bread crumbs
- 3 cups Mashed Potatoes (page 13); omit salt
- 2 eggs
- 1/4 cup grated Parmesan cheese
- 2 tablespoons minced parsley
- 1/8 teaspoon pepper
- 5 slices provolone cheese, divided

Preheat oven to 350°F. Butter a 6-cup ovenproof bowl. Add bread crumbs; shake bowl to coat inside with crumbs; set aside. Place potatoes in separate bowl. Beat in 1 egg at a time until smooth. Stir in Parmesan cheese, parsley, and pepper. Spoon one-third of the potato mixture into prepared bowl. Top with 2 slices provolone cheese. Spoon on remaining potato mixture. Top with remaining 3 slices cheese. Bake 1 hour, or until potatoes are golden brown and begin to pull away from edge of bowl. Loosen mold around edge with knife. Turn onto warm serving plate.

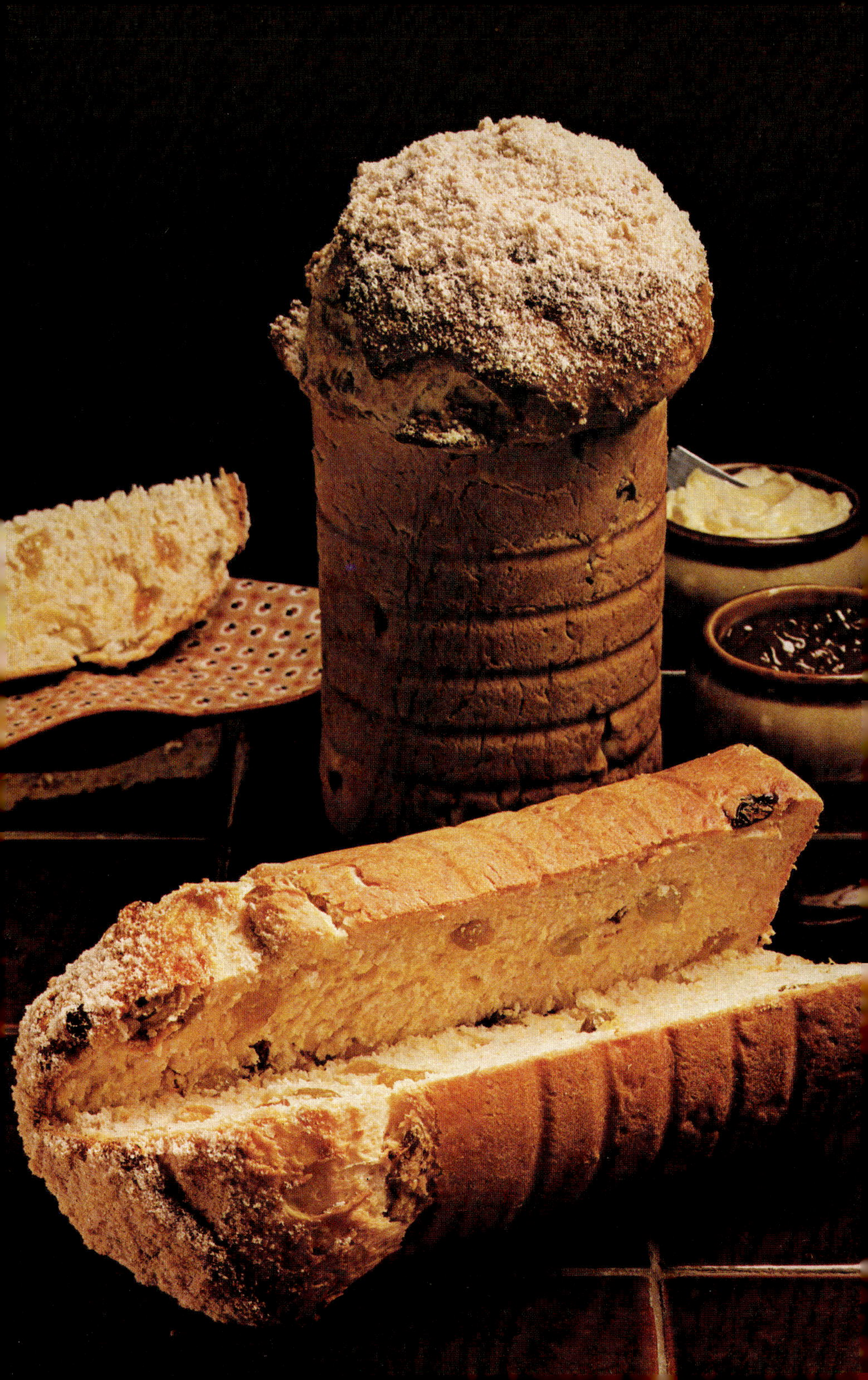

Babka (Polish Easter Bread) —— 1 large loaf

- 1 1/4 cups milk
- 1/2 cup butter or margarine
- 2 packages (1/4 ounce each) active dry yeast
- 7 to 7 1/2 cups all purpose flour, divided
- 1/2 cup sugar
- 1 teaspoon salt
- 1 cup Riced Potatoes (page 22)
- 4 eggs
- 1 egg, separated
- 1 tablespoon grated lemon peel
- 3/4 cup golden raisins
- 2 tablespoons all-purpose flour
- 2 tablespoons sugar
- 1/4 teaspoon cinnamon
- 2 teaspoons butter or margarine, softened

Heat milk and butter in small saucepan to 120°F to 130°F. Combine yeast, 3 cups flour, 1/2 cup sugar, salt, potatoes, 4 eggs, egg yolk, lemon peel, and warm milk-butter mixture in large bowl. Beat with electric mixer on high until smooth. Beat in 3 cups flour. Stir in raisins. Knead in enough remaining flour to form a soft dough. Place dough in lightly greased bowl; turn to coat entire surface. Cover and let rise in warm place, free from draft, until almost double in bulk, about 1 hour. Grease and flour 9-inch springform pan. Fold a 30-inch strip of aluminum foil lengthwise in half; grease one side of strip. Circle top of springform pan with foil, greased side in, extending 2 inches above rim of pan. Fasten ends with paper clips. Punch down dough. Shape into a ball. Place in prepared pan. Cover with oiled waxed paper. Let rise in warm place, free from draft, until dough is 3/4 inch from top of aluminum foil, about 40 minutes. Preheat oven to 350°F. Combine egg white and 1 tablespoon water in small bowl; mix with fork. Brush over top of bread. Combine 2 tablespoons flour, 2 tablespoons sugar, cinnamon, and butter in small bowl. Sprinkle over dough. Bake 50 to 60 minutes, or until golden brown. Cut into wedges and serve slightly warm.

You can also prepare Babka in two one-pound coffee cans. Grease cans as you would a baking pan. Bake as directed above.

Danish Glazed Potatoes — 8 to 10 servings

2 pounds small potatoes, washed
6 tablespoons sugar
3 tablespoons butter or margarine

Cook potatoes in salted boiling water about 15 minutes, or until almost tender. Drain; rinse in cold water. Peel; dry with paper towels; set aside. Heat sugar in heavy skillet over medium-high heat, stirring constantly, until light golden brown. Add butter; stir until completely blended. Add potatoes; remove skillet from heat. Roll potatoes with wooden spoon to coat with glaze. Serve hot. Potatoes can be reheated on low heat; stir and watch carefully to keep from burning.

French Beef Ragout — 8 servings

1/4 cup vegetable oil
2 pounds beef for stew, cut into 1-inch pieces
2 cups chopped onions
1 cup chopped celery
1 clove garlic, minced
1/3 cup all-purpose flour
1 can (16 ounces) tomatoes, undrained
1 cup dry white wine
2 cans (10 1/2 ounces each) beef bouillon
2 tablespoons minced parsley
1 teaspoon rosemary
1 bay leaf
1/2 teaspoon tarragon
2 teaspoons salt
1/4 teaspoon pepper
2 cups sliced carrots, cut into 1/2 inch slices
2 pounds small potatoes, washed and peeled
1 package (10 ounces) frozen peas, prepared according to package directions and drained

Heat oil in 6-quart Dutch oven; brown beef on all sides. Remove beef; set aside. Add onions, celery, and garlic; sauté about 5 minutes, or until onions are transparent. Remove pan from heat; stir in flour. Return pan to low heat; brown flour, stirring constantly, about 2 minutes. Add tomatoes with liquid, wine, bouillon, parsley, rosemary, bay leaf, tarragon, salt, and pepper. Bring to a boil. Add beef. Cover and simmer 2 to 3 hours, or until beef is tender. Skim off fat. Add carrots and potatoes. Simmer about 1 hour, or until vegetables are tender. Remove bay leaf. Sprinkle peas over stew. Serve hot.

Tex-Mex Green Chili Stew ——— 6 to 8 servings

- 1 tablespoon vegetable oil
- 1 pound boneless pork, cut into 1-inch pieces
- 1 large onion, chopped
- 4 medium potatoes, washed, peeled, and diced
- 2 cans (10 1/2 ounces each) chicken broth
- 2 cans (3 ounces each) whole green chilies, drained and diced
- 1/4 pound fresh mushrooms, sliced
- 2 teaspoons salt
- 1/4 teaspoon pepper
- 1 clove garlic, minced

Heat oil in Dutch oven. Add pork; brown on all sides. Add onion; cook until limp. Add remaining ingredients. Cover and simmer 3 to 3 1/2 hours. Ladle into soup bowls to serve.

This can be cooked in a slow cooker all day on low. Brown pork in skillet before adding to cooker.

Potato Kugel ——————————— 6 servings

- 3 large potatoes, washed, peeled, and grated
- 2 small onions, grated
- 2 eggs, slightly beaten
- 1/4 cup potato flour or matzo meal
- 2 teaspoons baking powder
- 1 teaspoon salt
- 1/4 teaspoon white pepper
- 6 tablespoons cold butter or margarine, divided

Preheat oven to 350°F. Grease a 9-inch pie plate; set aside. Drain potatoes on paper towels. Combine potatoes, onions, and egg in medium bowl; blend thoroughly. Combine flour, baking powder, salt, and pepper in separate bowl. Gradually stir flour mixture into potato mixture. Cut in 4 tablespoons butter. Spoon into prepared pie plate. Dot with remaining butter. Bake about 1 hour, or until top is crisp and golden brown. Cut into 6 wedges. Serve hot.

Potatoes can be shredded instead of grated, if desired.

Spanish Potatoes ———————————— 4 servings

- 2 tablespoons olive oil
- 1 large onion, thinly sliced
- 2 medium potatoes, washed, peeled, and thinly sliced
- 1 tablespoon minced pimiento
- 1/8 teaspoon saffron
- 1/2 teaspoon salt
- 1/3 cup sliced almonds

Heat oil in heavy 10-inch skillet. Sauté onion until limp. Add potatoes and pimiento; cook and stir until lightly browned. Combine saffron and salt; sprinkle on potatoes. Add 1 tablespoon water. Cover and cook about 15 minutes, stirring occasionally. Sprinkle with almonds. Serve hot.

Flemish Pork (Porc à la Flamande) ———————— 6 to 8 servings

- 2 tablespoons vegetable shortening
- 1 boneless pork shoulder (2 pounds), cubed
- 1 teaspoon salt
- 1/2 teaspoon pepper
- 2 cups beer
- 1/2 cup boiling water
- 1 teaspoon rosemary
- 12 small whole onions, peeled
- 2 cups beef bouillon
- 2 packages (10 ounces each) frozen Brussels sprouts, thawed
- 2 cups sliced cooked potatoes
- 2 cups sliced cooked carrots
- 1/4 cup all-purpose flour
- 1/2 cup cold water

Heat shortening in 4-quart Dutch oven on moderate heat. Add pork; brown on all sides. Sprinkle with salt and pepper. Add beer, boiling water, and rosemary. Simmer 45 minutes. Add onions; simmer 30 minutes. Stir in bouillon and Brussels sprouts. Cover and cook 10 minutes, or until Brussels sprouts are tender. Add potatoes and carrots. Blend flour with cold water in 1-cup measure. Slowly stir into pork mixture. Cook until thickened, stirring occasionally. Serve in soup bowls.

Moussaka

6 to 8 servings

- Peanut or corn oil for deep-fat frying
- 3 medium potatoes, peeled and cut into 1/4-inch slices
- 2 medium onions, chopped
- 1/4 cup olive oil
- 1 pound lean ground beef
- 2 cloves garlic, minced
- 1 can (8 ounces) tomato sauce
- 1 teaspoon cinnamon
- 1/2 teaspoon salt
- 1/8 teaspoon pepper
- 2 eggs
- 1 cup milk
- 1/2 cup grated Romano cheese

Preheat oven to 350°F. Heat 3 to 4 inches oil in deep-fat fryer or deep saucepan to 360°F. Fry potatoes until golden brown; drain on paper towels. Arrange half of the potatoes in even layer on bottom of shallow, 1 1/2-quart baking dish. Heat olive oil in skillet. Sauté onion until transparent. Remove onion with slotted spoon; set aside. Add beef to oil in skillet; cook and stir until no longer red. Drain fat. Add onion, garlic, tomato sauce, cinnamon, salt, and pepper to beef; blend well. Pour over potatoes. Arrange remaining potatoes over meat mixture. Combine eggs and milk in small bowl; blend well. Pour over casserole. Sprinkle with cheese. Bake 45 minutes. Cut into squares to serve.

To be truly Greek, this dish can be prepared using Kefalotyri cheese instead of Romano. You'll find it at specialty food stores and most cheese marts.

Irish Prairie Oaten

9 biscuits

- 1 cup quick-cooking oatmeal
- 2 cups Mashed Potatoes (page 13)
- 1/4 teaspoon salt
- 1/2 cup butter or margarine, melted
- 2 tablespoons butter or margarine

Place oatmeal in blender container or bowl of food processor; grind until fine. Combine oatmeal, potatoes, salt, and melted butter in mixing bowl; blend well to make a soft dough. Lightly cover working surface with additional oatmeal. Pat out dough to about 1-inch thickness. Use a 3-inch biscuit cutter to cut out 9 biscuits. Melt remaining 2 tablespoons butter in large skillet. Fry biscuits in butter, turning to brown both sides. Serve hot.

Cornish Pasty

6 servings

- 1 cup vegetable shortening
- 1 cup boiling water
- 4 cups all-purpose flour
- 1 teaspoon salt
- 3 large potatoes, washed, and peeled
- Ice water
- 2 medium onions, coarsely chopped
- 3/4 pound round steak, cut into 1/4-inch pieces
- 1/4 pound pork steak, cut into 1/4-inch pieces
- 1 large carrot, peeled and thinly sliced (about 1 cup)
- Salt and pepper
- 1/2 cup minced parsley
- 6 tablespoons butter or margarine, cut up

Place shortening in large bowl. Pour water over shortening; use fork to break up; stir until melted. Stir in flour and salt; blend well. Divide dough into 3 portions; shape each into a ball. Cover and let stand at room temperature 1 hour. Preheat oven to 350°F. Cut potatoes into small, irregular, chip-like pieces. (Do not slice or dice.) Place in bowl of ice water; set aside. Grease a baking sheet; set aside. Divide and shape dough into 6 balls. Roll out, 1 ball at a time, on lightly floured surface. Using a 9 or 10-inch plate as a guide, cut into circles. Remove potatoes from water; drain. Combine beef and pork in small bowl; mix lightly. Place about 1/4 cup potatoes on one half of dough circle; spoon 2 tablespoons onion over potatoes. Sprinkle lightly with salt and pepper. Place another 1/4 cup potatoes, 6 or 8 carrot slices, 2 tablespoons onion, and 1/3 cup meat mixture on top. Sprinkle lightly with salt and pepper. Top with 1 tablespoon parsley and 1 tablespoon butter. Stretch other half of pastry over filling to form a half circle; trim and flute edges. Place on prepared baking sheet. Repeat with remaining dough ingredients to make 6 pasties. Cut slits in top of each pasty to allow steam to escape. Bake 50 to 60 minutes, or until potatoes are tender and pastry golden brown. Serve hot or at room temperature. Pasties can be eaten with a fork or wrapped in a napkin and eaten like a sandwich.

Coarsely ground beef and pork can be substituted for cut up beef and pork. One cup chipped rutabaga can be substituted for carrot.

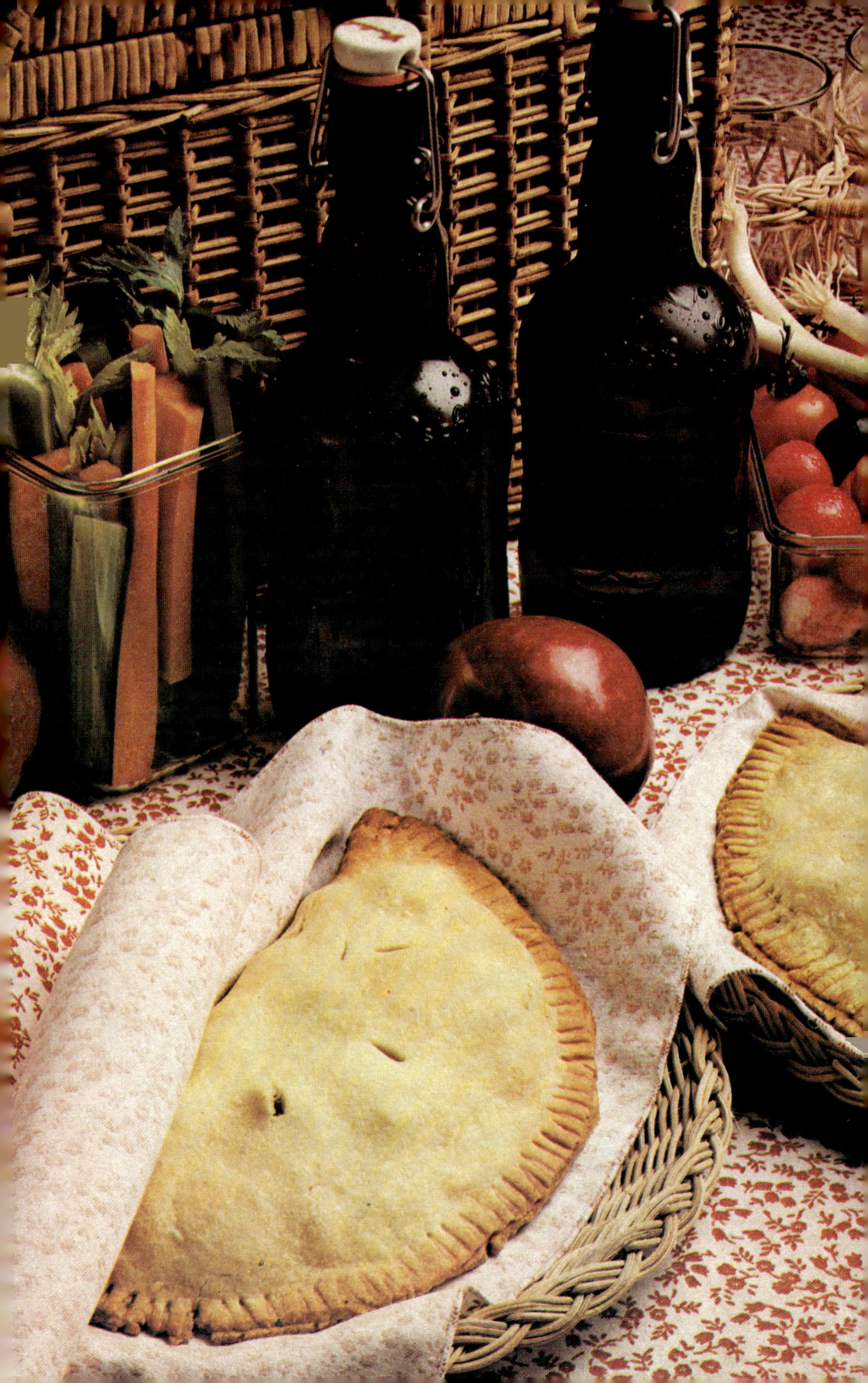

Russian Borscht —————————————— 10 servings

- 1 meaty beef soup bone
- 1/4 cup butter or margarine
- 2 carrots, peeled and sliced
- 3 stalks celery, sliced
- 4 medium onions, sliced, divided
- 2 large potatoes, washed, peeled, and halved
- 7 cups beef broth, divided
- 8 beets, cooked, peeled, and halved
- 1 can (29 ounces) tomatoes, undrained
- 1 bay leaf
- 2 cloves garlic
- 2 teaspoons salt
- 1/2 cup sherry
- 3 sprigs parsley
- 1 tablespoon sugar
- Dairy sour cream
- Dillweed

Remove meat from soup bone. Melt butter in large kettle; brown meat on all sides. Add carrots, celery, 3 onions, and potatoes; brown vegetables slightly. Add 4 cups beef broth; simmer 1 hour. Add 4 beets, tomatoes with liquid, bay leaf, garlic, salt, and sherry; simmer 4 hours. Cool to room temperature; cover and refrigerate at least 8 hours or overnight. Skim off fat with slotted spoon. Remove meat and vegetables; strain soup. Return stock to kettle. Add remaining 4 beets, 3 cups beef broth, parsley, sugar, and 1 onion; simmer 2 hours. Skim off fat; strain. Serve hot, garnished with dollop of sour cream and pinch of dillweed.

Vichyssoise —————————————————— 8 servings

- 1/2 cup water
- 6 leeks (white part only), thinly sliced
- 1 medium onion, thinly sliced
- 1 stalk celery, diced
- 4 cups chicken broth
- 5 medium potatoes, washed, peeled, and diced
- 2 cups milk, heated
- 1 teaspoon salt
- 1/4 teaspoon white pepper
- 1 cup half-and-half
- Chopped chives

Heat water in large saucepan. Add leek, onion, and celery; cook 5 minutes. Add broth and potatoes; simmer 15 minutes. Add milk; bring just to a boil. Remove from heat. Stir in salt and pepper. Place, 2 cups at a time, in blender container or bowl of food processor; purée. Chill thoroughly. Stir in half-and-half. Serve in chilled cups or soup bowls. Garnish each serving with chopped chives.

Roesti (Swiss Fried Potato) ──── 4 servings

- 6 medium potatoes, washed, cooked, peeled, and chilled
- 2 tablespoons butter or margarine
- 3 tablespoons vegetable shortening
- 1/3 cup chopped onion
- 1 teaspoon salt

Coarsely shred potatoes; set aside. Heat butter and shortening in heavy skillet. Sauté onion until limp, but not brown. Add potatoes and salt. Use spoon or spatula to shape mixture loosely into a cake. Fry about 20 minutes, turning occasionally with spatula, until golden brown. Turn out onto serving plate. Cut in quarters to serve.

Bigos (Polish Pork Stew) ──── 6 to 8 servings

- 1 can (16 ounces) sauerkraut
- 2 cups beef broth
- 1 can (16 ounces) tomatoes, drained; reserve liquid
- 1 tablespoon bacon fat
- 1 cup chopped onions
- 1 large apple, peeled, cored, and chopped
- 1 pound smoked Kielbasa, cut into 1-inch pieces
- 2 cups diced cooked pork
- 1/2 teaspoon salt
- 1/8 teaspoon pepper
- Dash cayenne
- 1 tablespoon sugar
- 1 tablespoon all-purpose flour
- 2 cups sliced fresh mushrooms
- 2 pounds potatoes, washed

Rinse and drain sauerkraut. Combine sauerkraut, broth, and liquid from tomatoes in heavy 4-quart saucepan; simmer 20 minutes. Heat bacon fat in large skillet. Sauté onions until limp. Add tomatoes, apple, and Kielbasa; cook just until heated. Stir in pork; simmer 10 minutes. Stir in salt, pepper, cayenne, sugar, and flour. Add mushrooms. Cook and stir until slightly thickened. Add sauerkraut; simmer 1 1/2 to 2 hours, adding more broth if mixture becomes too dry. Refrigerate at least 8 hours, or overnight. Reheat slowly. Peel potatoes; cut in half. Boil in salted water until tender, about 20 minutes; drain. To serve, ladle pork stew over hot potatoes.

Potato Knishes ———————— 6 servings

- 1/2 cup plus 2 tablespoons all-purpose flour
- 1 1/2 teaspoons sugar
- Dash salt
- 2 tablespoons vegetable oil
- 1 1/2 tablespoons lukewarm water
- 1 egg, slightly beaten
- 1 1/2 cups Mashed Potatoes (page 13)
- 1/3 cup minced onion
- 2 tablespoons butter or margarine, melted
- 1/2 teaspoon salt
- 1/8 teaspoon pepper
- Vegetable oil

Preheat oven to 350°F. Grease a baking sheet; set aside. Combine flour, sugar, and dash salt in medium bowl. Add 2 tablespoons oil, water, and egg; blend thoroughly. Turn dough out onto lightly floured surface. Knead dough 5 minutes. Roll out into 6 × 18-inch rectangle. Using greased knife, cut lengthwise into 2 equal strips. Combine potatoes, onion, butter, 1/2 teaspoon salt, and pepper in medium bowl. Spread half of the potato mixture evenly over 1 strip dough. Top with remaining strip. Moisten edges with water; seal. Cut into 1 1/2-inch slices. Place on prepared baking sheet. Brush with oil. Bake 30 to 35 minutes, or until brown. Makes a delicious accompaniment to a meat and gravy main dish.

Italian Omelet (Frittata di Sausage) ———————— 6 servings

- 1/2 pound Italian sausage, cut into 1/2-inch slices
- 1/2 cup chopped onion
- 1/2 large green pepper, seeded and cut into thin strips
- 3 medium potatoes, washed, peeled, and sliced (3 cups)
- 4 large eggs

Sauté sausage in large skillet on moderate heat until no longer pink. Add onion and green pepper; cook until vegetables are limp. Add potatoes. Cover and cook 10 minutes, or until potatoes are tender, stirring occasionally. Beat eggs and 4 tablespoons water in small bowl. Pour egg mixture evenly over potatoes. Cook on low heat about 5 minutes, or until eggs are set. To serve, either cut into wedges or spoon into serving dish.

Creamy Dutch Potatoes ——————— 4 servings

- 1 medium onion, sliced
- 1 tablespoon butter or margarine
- 2 cups washed, peeled, and diced potatoes
- 1/2 teaspoon salt
- Dash pepper
- 1 tablespoon minced parsley
- 3/4 cup boiling water
- 1 tablespoon cold water
- 2 teaspoons all-purpose flour

Melt butter on moderate heat in 9-inch skillet. Sauté onion until transparent. Add potatoes, salt, pepper, and parsley; stir. Stir in boiling water. Cover; simmer about 20 minutes, or until potatoes are tender. Blend cold water and flour in measuring cup. Stir into potato mixture. Bring to a boil; cook 2 minutes, stirring constantly, until slightly thickened.

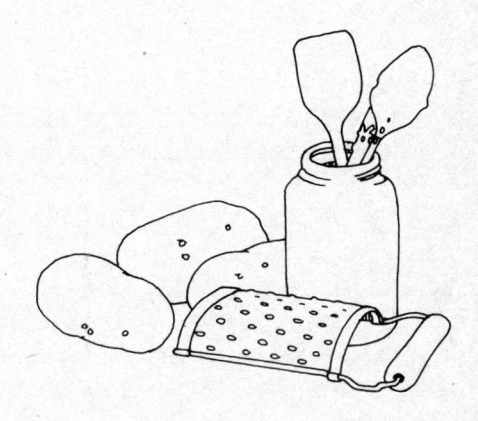

Scottish Scones ——————— 4 to 6 servings

- 2 cups packaged biscuit mix
- 4 tablespoons instant potato flakes
- 2 tablespoons sugar
- 1 egg
- 1 cup buttermilk
- 6 tablespoons butter or margarine, melted, divided

Preheat oven to 400°F. Grease an 8-inch square pan; set aside. Combine biscuit mix, potato flakes, and sugar in medium bowl. Combine egg, buttermilk, and 3 tablespoons butter in small bowl; blend well. Add to dry ingredients; stir until blended. Spoon into prepared pan; pat evenly over bottom. Brush generously with remaining butter. Bake 25 minutes, or until golden brown. Cut into squares. Split and serve with butter and jam or honey.

Gnocci
5 to 6 servings

- 3 medium potatoes, washed
- 2 egg yolks
- 1/2 teaspoon salt
- 1 cup all-purpose flour
- 1 tablespoon vegetable oil
- 1 1/2 cups canned or homemade spaghetti sauce, divided
- 1 cup grated Parmesan cheese, divided

Cook potatoes in medium saucepan 25 minutes, or until tender. Let cool; peel and rice. (You should have about 3 cups.) Combine potatoes, egg yolks, and salt in medium bowl; beat with electric mixer until evenly yellow. Add flour; blend well. Turn out onto lightly floured surface. Knead until smooth. Add more flour, a little at at time, if dough is too sticky. Divide dough into 6 portions. Shape each into 1/2-inch diameter roll. Cut roll into 1-inch pieces. Press each with fork to flatten. Sprinkle lightly with flour. Let stand 3 to 4 hours to rest. Bring 4 quarts lightly salted water to a boil in 6-quart kettle; add oil. Add about half of the gnocci to boiling water. Cook 5 minutes until gnocci floats on top of water and is tender. Remove with slotted spoon to heated bowl; keep warm. Repeat for remaining gnocci. Add 1 cup spaghetti sauce and 2/3 cup cheese to gnocci; toss to coat. Turn out onto serving platter. Top with remaining spaghetti sauce. Sprinkle with remaining cheese.

To serve gnocci as a side dish, drain and place in serving dish. Drizzle on 2 tablespoons olive oil. Sprinkle with 1/3 cup grated Parmesan cheese or 1/2 cup shredded Mozzarella cheese. Toss lightly to coat.

One Potato-
Two Potato-
Three Potato- Four

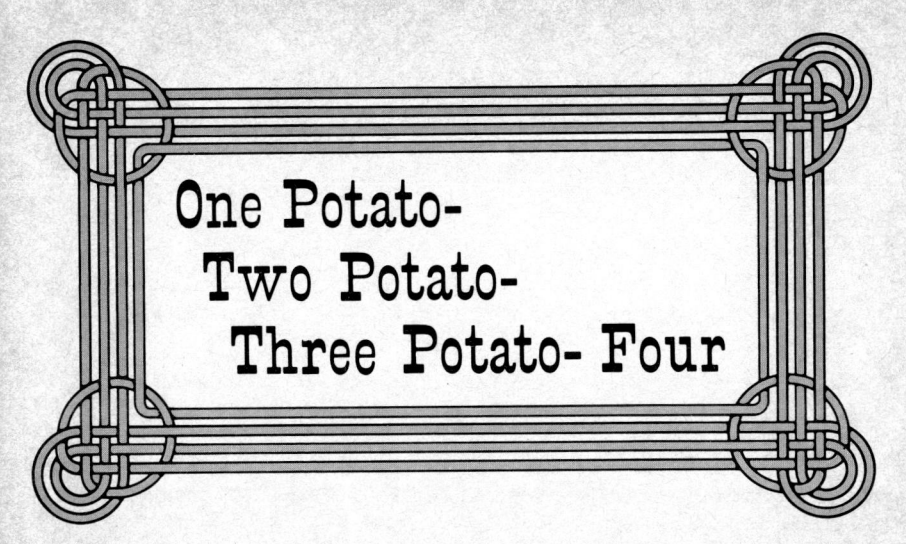

A fun thing happened on the way to the kitchen. The show-off potato became a candy, and a cookie, not to mention a nest and a pretzel. The recipes in this chapter were hand-picked to illustrate the potato's chameleon-like character and to show that the spud has a sense of humor. Go ahead and make some fun.

Coconut Pecan Balls — 5 dozen

- 1 package (16 ounces) confectioners sugar
- 4 cups flaked coconut
- 3/4 cup Mashed Potatoes (page 13), chilled
- 1/2 cup finely chopped pecans
- 1 teaspoon almond extract
- 1 package (14.3 ounces) chocolate fudge frosting mix
- 2 tablespoons butter or margarine
- 2 tablespoons light corn syrup

Combine sugar, coconut, potatoes, pecans, and almond extract in large bowl; blend thoroughly. Drop by heaping teaspoonfuls onto waxed paper-lined baking sheet. Chill 1 hour. Roll each drop into a 1-inch ball; set aside. Combine frosting mix, 3 tablespoons water, butter, and corn syrup in top of double boiler. Place top over boiling water; heat and stir until smooth. Dip balls into frosting mixture, swirling to coat evenly. Remove with tongs or fork to waxed paper-lined baking sheet. Chill 1 hour, or until coating hardens. Store in airtight container.

Chocolate Covered Potato Candy ──────── 40 pieces

    1 package (16 ounces) confectioners sugar
    4 cups flaked coconut
    3/4 cup Mashed Potatoes (page 13), chilled
    1 teaspoon almond extract
    1 package (6 ounces) semisweet chocolate pieces
    4 squares (1 ounce each) semisweet chocolate
    1/3 bar (2 1/2 × 1 1/2 inches) paraffin

Combine sugar, coconut, potatoes, and almond extract in large bowl; blend well. Drop by heaping teaspoonfuls onto waxed paper-lined baking sheet. Chill 1 hour. Roll each drop into a ball; set aside. Combine chocolate pieces, squares, and paraffin in top of double boiler. Place top over boiling water; heat until chocolate and paraffin are melted, stirring constantly. Dip coconut balls into chocolate mixture, swirling to coat evenly. Remove with tongs or fork to waxed paper-lined baking sheet. Chill 1 hour, or until coating hardens. Store in airtight container.

Potato-Peanut Butter Roll ──────── 1 roll

    1 package (32 ounces) confectioners sugar
    2/3 cup Mashed Potatoes (page 13), chilled
    2 tablespoons butter or margarine, softened
    1 teaspoon vanilla
    1 jar (18 ounces) creamy peanut butter

Combine sugar, potatoes, butter, and vanilla in large bowl; blend thoroughly. Shape into a ball. Place between two pieces oiled waxed paper. Roll out into 9 × 14-inch rectangle. Spread peanut butter evenly over rectangle. Roll up from short side. Wrap in waxed paper. Chill 2 hours. Cut into 1/2-inch slices to serve.

Potato-Coconut Bar Roll ———————— 1 roll

2 1/2 cups flaked coconut
1 3/4 cups confectioners sugar
   1/3 cup Mashed Potatoes
      (page 13), chilled
1/2 teaspoon vanilla
1/2 cup semisweet chocolate
   pieces, melted

Combine coconut, sugar, potatoes, and vanilla in large bowl; blend well. Shape into roll about 1 1/2 inches in diameter. Spread chocolate on roll. Chill 2 hours. Cut into 1/2-inch slices to serve.

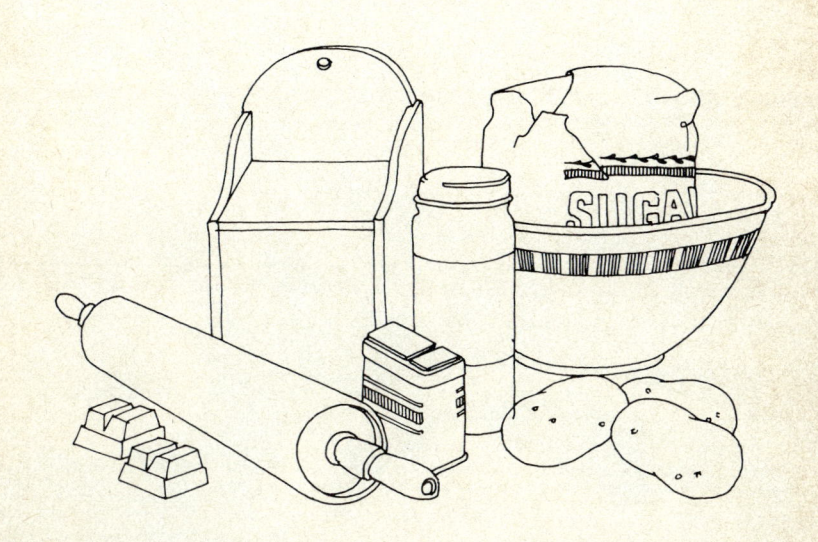

Potato Chip Cookies ———————— 3 1/2 dozen

   3 cups all-purpose flour
   1 cup sugar
   1 cup crushed potato chips
   2 egg yolks
   3/4 cup vegetable shortening
1/2 cup butter or margarine,
   softened
1 teaspoon vanilla
Confectioners sugar

Combine flour, sugar, chips, egg yolks, shortening, butter, and vanilla in large bowl; beat with electric mixer until mixture is consistency of fine crumbs. Preheat oven to 350°F. Shape dough into 1 to 1 1/2-inch balls; place on ungreased baking sheet. Flatten balls with bottom of glass. Bake 10 to 12 minutes, or until very lightly browned. Remove from baking sheet; cool. Dust with confectioners sugar.

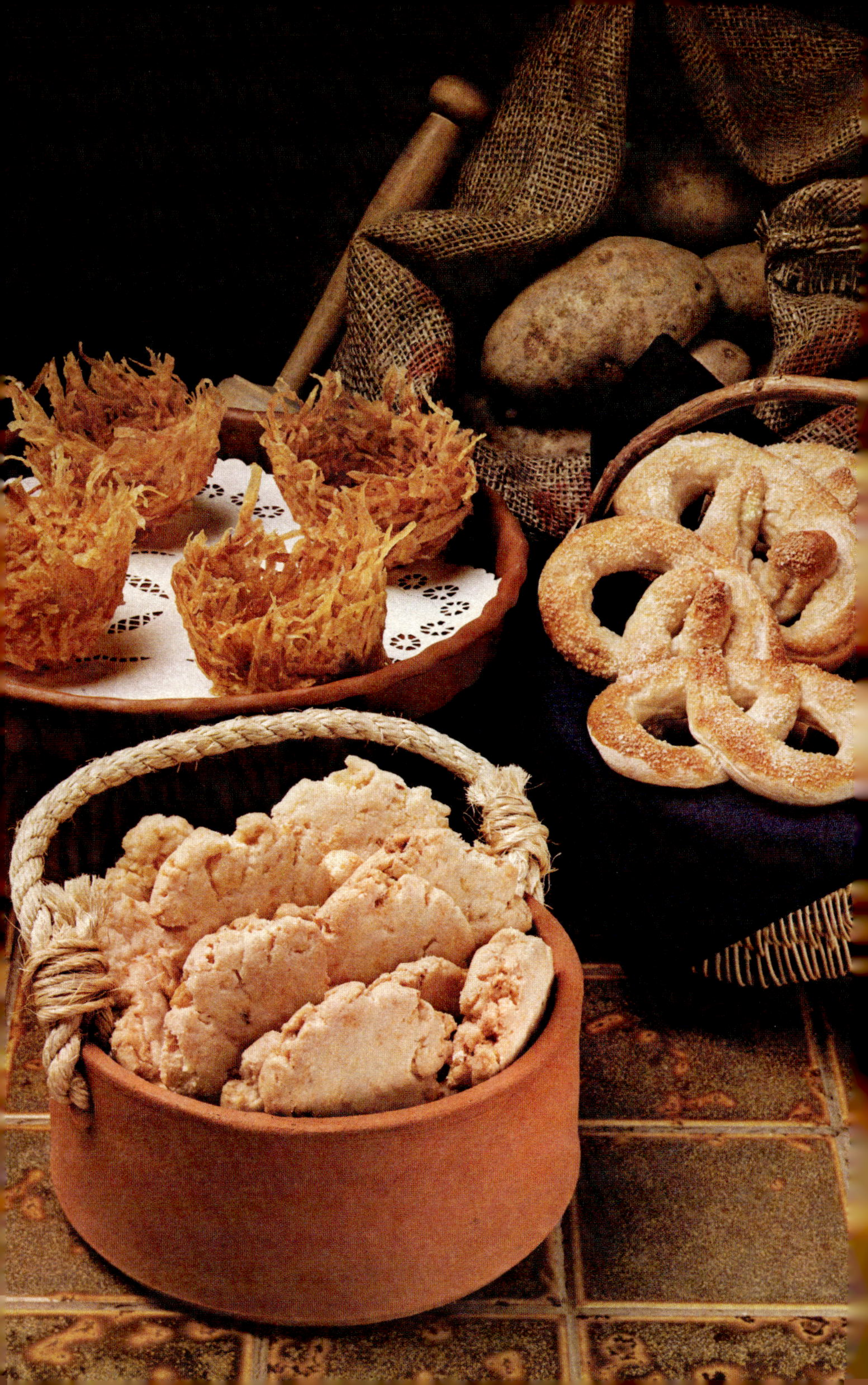

Soft Potato Pretzels _____ 6 servings

1 medium potato, washed, peeled, cooked, and mashed; reserve 1 1/2 cups potato water
3 1/2 to 4 cups all-purpose flour, divided
1 package (1/4 ounce) active dry yeast
1 teaspoon salt
1 teaspoon sugar
1 egg, slightly beaten
2 teaspoons coarse salt

Heat reserved potato water in small saucepan to 120°F to 130°F. Combine 2 cups flour, warm potato water, potato, yeast, salt, and sugar in large bowl. Beat with electric mixer on high 2 minutes. Stir in remaining flour. Turn dough out onto lightly floured surface. Knead 5 minutes, or until dough is smooth and elastic. Place in lightly greased bowl; turn to coat entire surface. Cover and let rise in warm place, free from draft, until almost double in bulk, about 1 hour. Punch dough down. Preheat oven to 425°F. Divide dough into 12 to 14 parts. Roll each part into a rope; twist into pretzel shapes. Place on ungreased baking sheet. Brush with egg. Sprinkle with coarse salt. Bake 20 to 25 minutes, or until golden brown. Serve immediately. Store remaining pretzels in container with loose fitting cover.

Potato Nests (page 136), Soft Potato Pretzels, Potato Chip Cookies (page 133)

Potato Nests

Peanut or corn oil for
   deep-fat frying
Potatoes, washed and
   peeled

Ice water
Nest mold

Preheat oil in deep-fat fryer to 390°F. Use shredder to cut potatoes into 1/4-inch strips, or cut as for Shoestring Potatoes (page 21). Soak potatoes in ice water 30 minutes. Drain well; dry on paper towels. Dip the special nest mold fry basket into hot oil. Fill the large basket with 3/4 to 1 cup potatoes. Line the basket with potatoes. Insert smaller basket; clamp together. Fry nests 3 to 4 minutes, or until golden brown and crisp. Remove from oil; unmold; drain on paper towels. Repeat for remaining potatoes. Fill the baskets with creamed foods such as Chicken à la King (page 95) or Creamed Ham and Peas (page 93). If baskets are not filled immediately, reheat briefly in oven.

If you do not have the special nest mold, two metal strainers can be successfully used. Use care to avoid hot oil splatters. One strainer should be 3 inches in diameter, the other somewhat smaller. Long handles are helpful, but not essential.

Crispy Pecan Cookies — 3 1/2 dozen

2 cups firmly packed light
   brown sugar
1 cup vegetable shortening
2 eggs
1 teaspoon vanilla

2 cups all-purpose flour
1 teaspoon baking soda
1 1/2 cups crushed potato chips
1/2 cup chopped pecans
Sugar

Cream sugar and shortening in large bowl with electric mixer until fluffy. Add eggs and vanilla; beat until well mixed. Add flour, baking soda, and chips; mix well. Stir in pecans. Shape into walnut-size balls. Place on ungreased baking sheet. Flatten balls with bottom of glass dipped in sugar. Bake 12 to 15 minutes. Remove from baking sheet to cool.

Coconut Chip Cookies ———————— 4 dozen

- 1/2 cup butter or margarine, softened
- 1/2 cup sugar
- 1/2 cup firmly packed light brown sugar
- 1 egg
- 1/2 teaspoon vanilla
- 1 cup crushed Potato Chips (page 18)
- 1 cup all-purpose flour
- 1/2 cup flaked coconut
- 1/2 teaspoon baking soda
- 1/2 cup semisweet chocolate pieces
- 1/4 cup chopped peanuts

Preheat oven to 350°F. Cream butter, sugars, egg, and vanilla in large bowl with electric mixer until fluffy. Add chips, flour, coconut, and baking soda; blend well. Stir in chocolate pieces and peanuts. Shape into walnut-size balls. Place on ungreased baking sheet. Bake 10 to 12 minutes. Remove from baking sheet to cool.

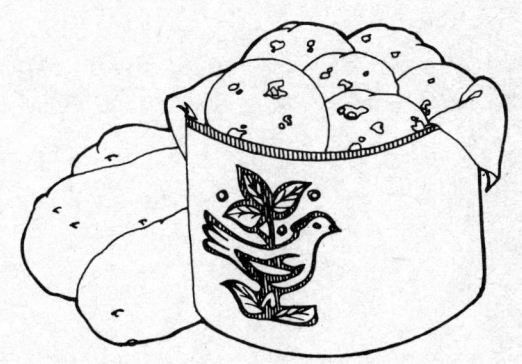

Spicy Cocoa Cookies ———————— 3 1/2 to 4 dozen

- 1 1/2 cups sugar
- 1/2 cup vegetable shortening
- 2 eggs
- 1 cup Mashed Potatoes (page 13), chilled
- 2 cups all-purpose flour
- 2 tablespoons cocoa
- 1 teaspoon cinnamon
- 1 teaspoon baking powder
- 1/2 teaspoon nutmeg

Preheat oven to 350°F. Grease a baking sheet; set aside. Cream sugar and shortening in large bowl with electric mixer until fluffy. Add eggs and potatoes; blend well. Combine flour, cocoa, cinnamon, baking powder, and nutmeg in separate bowl. Add to creamed mixture; blend well. Drop by rounded tablespoonfuls onto prepared baking sheet. Bake 10 to 12 minutes. Remove from baking sheet to cool.

Chocolate Potato Drop Cookies ———————— 4 1/2 dozen

- 1 cup firmly packed light brown sugar
- 1/2 cup butter or margarine, softened
- 1 teaspoon vanilla
- 1 egg
- 2 cups all-purpose flour
- 1/2 teaspoon salt
- 1/2 teaspoon baking soda
- 1/2 cup Mashed Potatoes (page 13), chilled
- 3/4 cup buttermilk
- 2 squares (1 ounce each) unsweetened chocolate, melted
- 1/2 cup chopped nuts

Preheat oven to 375°F. Cream sugar, butter, and vanilla in large bowl with electric mixer until fluffy. Add egg; beat well. Combine flour, salt, and baking soda in separate bowl; set aside. Beat potatoes into creamed mixture. Alternately beat in dry ingredients and milk. Add chocolate; blend well. Stir in nuts. Drop by large tablespoonfuls onto ungreased baking sheet. Bake 12 to 13 minutes. Remove from baking sheet to cool. Dust with confectioners sugar, if desired.

Raisin Drop Cookies ———————— 4 dozen

- 1 cup sugar
- 1/3 cup vegetable oil
- 2 eggs
- 1 cup Riced Potatoes (page 22), at room temperature
- 1 cup all-purpose flour
- 3 teaspoons baking powder
- 2 squares (1 ounce each) semisweet chocolate, melted
- 1/3 cup raisins

Preheat oven to 350°F. Grease a baking sheet; set aside. Combine sugar, oil, and eggs in large bowl; beat with electric mixer until smooth. Add potatoes; blend well. Add flour and baking powder; blend well. Add chocolate; blend thoroughly. Stir in raisins. Drop by heaping tablespoonfuls onto prepared baking sheet. Bake 10 to 12 minutes. Remove from baking sheet to cool.

Almond Bars _____ 36 bars

- 2 cups all-purpose flour
- 3/4 cup sugar
- 3/4 cup butter or margarine, softened
- 1 teaspoon baking powder
- 1 teaspoon salt
- 2 cups ground almonds
- 1 1/4 cups confectioners sugar
- 1/2 cup Mashed Potatoes (page 13), at room temperature
- 3 eggs
- 1 teaspoon cinnamon
- 1/2 teaspoon cardamom
- Confectioners sugar

Preheat oven to 375°F. Combine flour, sugar, butter, baking powder, and salt in large bowl; beat with electric mixer until mixture is consistency of fine crumbs. Press into bottom of ungreased 9 × 13-inch baking pan. Bake 10 minutes. While crust is baking, combine almonds, confectioners sugar, potatoes, eggs, cinnamon, and cardamom in large bowl; blend well. Pour mixture over hot crust. Return to oven. Bake 20 to 25 minutes, or until golden brown. Place pan on wire rack. Cool completely in pan before cutting into bars. Dust lightly with confectioners sugar.

Bread Torte _____ 8 servings

- 6 eggs, separated
- 1 cup sugar
- 1 cup finely chopped almonds
- 3/4 cup fine dry bread crumbs
- 1/2 cup Riced Potatoes (page 22), at room temperature
- 1/4 teaspoon cinnamon
- 1/4 cup white wine

Preheat oven to 350°F. Grease and flour a 9-inch springform pan; set aside. Beat egg whites in small bowl with electric mixer until stiff peaks form; set aside. Beat egg yolks and sugar in large mixing bowl until lemon-colored. Add almonds, bread crumbs, potatoes, cinnamon, and wine; beat until well mixed. Carefully fold in egg whites until white is no longer visible. Pour into prepared pan. Bake 1 hour. Cool completely before releasing side of pan. (Cake will fall slightly during cooling.) Serve in wedges, topped with your favorite dessert sauce.

Almond Chocolate Torte
_____ 12 servings

- 2 cups sugar
- 1 cup butter or margarine, softened
- 4 eggs, separated
- 1 cup Riced Potatoes (page 22)
- 1 1/2 cups cake flour
- 4 squares (1 ounce each) unsweetened chocolate, grated
- 2 teaspoons baking powder
- 1 teaspoon cinnamon
- 1/4 teaspoon ground cloves
- 1/2 cup half-and-half
- 1 teaspoon vanilla
- 1 teaspoon grated lemon peel
- 1 cup chopped almonds

Preheat oven to 325°F. Grease a 9-inch springform pan; set aside. Cream sugar, butter, and egg yolks in large bowl with electric mixer until smooth. Add potatoes; blend well. Combine flour, chocolate, baking powder, cinnamon, and cloves in separate bowl. Alternately beat in dry ingredients and half-and-half to sugar-butter mixture until well mixed. Stir in vanilla, lemon peel, and almonds. Beat egg whites in small bowl with electric mixer until stiff peaks form. Carefully fold egg whites into chocolate mixture until white is no longer visible. Pour into prepared pan. Bake 1 hour and 15 minutes, or until toothpick inserted in center comes out clean. Cool completely in pan before releasing side of pan. Serve with ice cream or topped with a favorite sauce.

Whipped Cream Potato Torte

12 servings

- 4 eggs, separated
- 1 cup sugar, divided
- 1 cup all-purpose flour
- 1 cup finely chopped pecans
- 1 cup Mashed Potatoes (page 13), at room temperature
- 1 teaspoon grated orange peel
- 1/2 teaspoon salt
- 1/2 teaspoon baking powder
- 1 1/2 cups heavy cream
- 5 tablespoons sugar
- 5 teaspoons cocoa, divided

Preheat oven to 325°F. Grease and flour a 9-inch springform pan; set aside. Beat egg whites and 1/4 cup sugar in small bowl with electric mixer until stiff peaks form; set aside. Beat egg yolks and remaining 3/4 cup sugar in large bowl until thick and lemon-colored. Stir in flour, pecans, potatoes, orange peel, salt, and baking powder; blend until smooth. Carefully fold in egg whites. Pour into prepared pan. Bake 1 hour, or until toothpick inserted in center comes out clean. Cool torte completely in pan on wire rack before releasing side of pan. Beat cream, 5 tablespoons sugar, and 4 1/2 teaspoons cocoa in small bowl with electric mixer until stiff. Release sides of pan. Remove torte. Spread cream over top of torte. Sprinkle with remaining 1/2 teaspoon cocoa. Refrigerate until ready to serve.

Potato Crust

2 9-inch crusts

- 2 cups all-purpose flour
- 1/2 teaspoon salt
- 2 teaspoons baking powder
- 1/2 cup vegetable shortening
- 1 cup Mashed Potatoes (page 13), chilled
- 4 to 5 tablespoons cold milk

Preheat oven to 350°F. Sift flour, salt, and baking powder into large bowl. Cut in shortening. Add potatoes; blend well. Add enough milk, 1 tablespoon at a time, to form a soft dough. Divide and shape into 2 balls. Roll out on lightly floured surface to fit pie plate. Ease into pie plate. Prick bottom and sides of shell with fork. Bake 15 minutes.

Can be used for meat pies, quiche, or pizza. Use dough immediately; it does not store well.

Potato Chip Apple Crisp — 6 servings

- 2 cups finely crushed potato chips
- 1/4 cup confectioners sugar
- 1/4 cup whole-wheat flour
- 1 tablespoon grated lemon peel
- 1 tablespoon vegetable oil
- 1/2 teaspoon cinnamon
- 1/4 teaspoon nutmeg
- 5 large tart apples, pared, cored, and sliced
- 3/4 cup sugar
- 1 tablespoon all-purpose flour
- 1/4 cup oatmeal

Preheat oven to 375°F. Combine chips, confectioners sugar, flour, lemon peel, and oil in small bowl; blend well. Press all but 1/2 cup of the chip mixture into bottom and sides of 8-inch square baking pan. Combine cinnamon and nutmeg in large bowl. Add apples, sugar, and flour, to cinnamon-nutmeg mixture; toss to coat apples. Place apples in prepared crust. Combine oatmeal and reserved chip mixture in small bowl; sprinkle over apples. Bake 30 minutes, or until apples are tender and topping is golden. Serve warm topped with ice cream.

When Time is Short

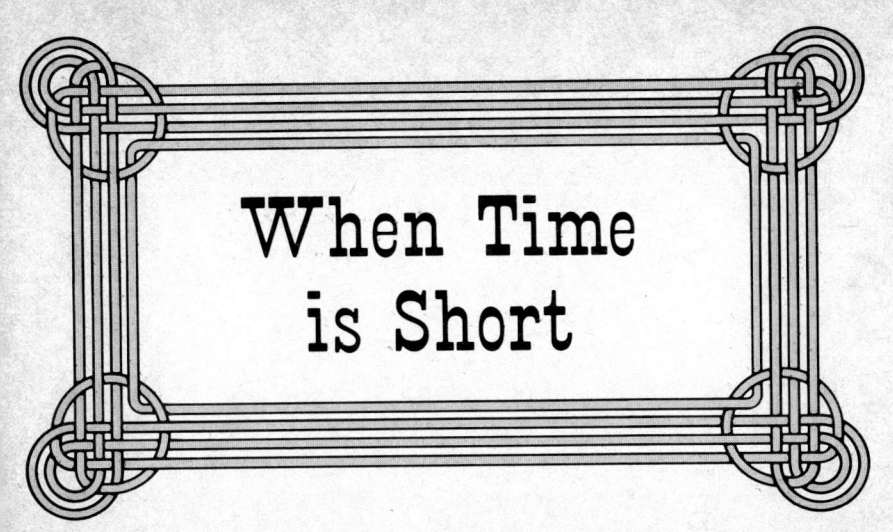

Forget to plan supper? Only an hour before the gang arrives? Then it's time to take advantage of those magnificent, but often ill-used, convenience food products. Spur-of-the-moment anxiety will become spud-of-the-moment satisfaction. And, best of all, no one will know dehydrated, canned, or frozen potatoes helped you out!

Salisbury Skillet Supper — 4 servings

1 1/2 pounds lean ground beef
1 can (5.3 ounces) evaporated milk, undiluted
1 egg, slightly beaten
1 cup soft bread crumbs (2 slices)
1/2 teaspoon salt
1 tablespoon onion flakes
1 tablespoon vegetable oil
1 can (16 ounces) sliced potatoes, drained; reserve liquid
1 package (10 ounces) frozen peas
1 can (4 ounces) sliced mushrooms, undrained
1 envelope (1 5/8 ounces) onion soup mix

Combine beef, milk, egg, bread crumbs, salt, and onion flakes in large bowl; blend thoroughly. Shape into 4 large 1-inch thick oval patties. Heat oil in 10-inch skillet on moderate heat. Add patties; brown on both sides. Drain, if necessary. Add enough water to reserved potato liquid to equal 1 cup. Add potatoes, peas, mushrooms, soup mix, and 1 cup potato liquid to beef mixture. Heat to a boil; simmer, covered, 20 minutes, stirring once during cooking to blend.

Hot German Potato Supper _____ 4 servings

- 5 slices bacon, cut into 1/2-inch pieces
- 1 can (10 1/2 ounces) cream of celery soup, undiluted
- 2 tablespoons sweet pickle relish
- 2 tablespoons vinegar
- 2 tablespoons onion flakes
- 1 tablespoon diced pimiento
- 1 can (16 ounces) sliced potatoes, drained
- 1 can (12 ounces) luncheon meat, sliced
- Minced parsley

Fry bacon in skillet until crisp. Remove bacon with slotted spoon; drain on paper towels; crumble; set aside. Pour off all but 1 tablespoon drippings from skillet. Stir soup, relish, vinegar, onion flakes, and pimiento into drippings. Cook, stirring constantly, until mixture comes to a boil. Reduce heat. Stir in potatoes and bacon. Arrange meat slices on top of potato mixture. Cover and simmer 8 to 10 minutes, or until heated through. Garnish with parsley.

Hamburger Pie _____ 6 servings

- 1 1/2 pounds lean ground beef
- 1/4 cup onion flakes
- 1 egg, beaten
- 1 dozen buttery crackers, crumbled
- 1 tablespoon parsley flakes
- 1 teaspoon seasoned salt
- 1/4 teaspoon pepper
- 6 slices process American cheese
- 2 cups instant mashed potatoes, prepared according to package directions
- Paprika

Preheat oven to 350°F. Combine beef, onion, egg, cracker crumbs, parsley, salt, and pepper in large bowl. Pat into 9-inch pie pan; cover with aluminum foil and bake 45 minutes, or until done; drain. Arrange cheese over beef mixture and spread mashed potatoes carefully over cheese. Sprinkle with paprika. Cook, uncovered, 10 to 15 minutes. Cut into wedges to serve.

Tater-Hamburger Casserole ──── 4 servings

- 1 pound lean ground beef
- 1 medium onion, chopped
- 1/2 teaspoon salt
- 1/8 teaspoon pepper
- 1 teaspoon Worcestershire sauce
- 1 can (12 ounces) whole-kernel corn, drained
- 1 package (16 ounces) frozen potato tots
- 1 can (10 3/4 ounces) cream of mushroom soup, undiluted
- Milk

Preheat oven to 350°F. Combine beef, onion, salt, and pepper in large skillet; brown on moderate heat, stirring frequently to break up beef; drain fat. Spoon into 2-quart casserole. Stir in Worcestershire and corn. Arrange potato tots on top. Blend soup with 1/2 soup can milk in small bowl. Pour over top of casserole. Bake, uncovered, 45 to 60 minutes, or until heated through.

Browned Potatoes in Cream ──── 2 servings

- 1 tablespoon butter or margarine
- 1 can (8 ounces) sliced potatoes, drained
- 1/4 teaspoon onion salt
- Dash white pepper
- 1/4 cup half-and-half

Heat butter in small, heavy skillet over low heat. Add potatoes, onion, salt, and pepper. Cook until potatoes are golden brown, stirring occasionally. Stir in half-and-half. Simmer, uncovered, 2 minutes.

Garlic-Parsley Potato Balls ──── 2 servings

- 1 tablespoon butter or margarine
- 1 can (8 ounces) whole potatoes, drained
- 1 clove garlic, minced
- 1/4 teaspoon salt
- 1 teaspoon minced parsley

Melt butter in small, heavy skillet on low heat. Add potatoes, garlic, and salt. Cook until potatoes are golden brown, stirring occasionally. Sprinkle with parsley.

Quick Sausage-Vegie Stew ———— 6 servings

- 2 tablespoons cornstarch
- 1 tablespoon instant minced onion
- 1 teaspoon instant chicken bouillon granules
- 1/2 teaspoon basil
- 1/4 teaspoon salt
- 1 can (16 ounces) stewed tomatoes, undrained
- 1 can (16 ounces) sliced carrots, drained
- 1 teaspoon Worcestershire sauce
- 12 ounces cooked fresh Kielbasa, cut into 1/2-inch slices
- 1 can (16 ounces) sliced potatoes, drained
- 1/4 cup chopped celery
- 1 tablespoon minced parsley
- 1 package (7.5 ounces) refrigerated buttermilk biscuit dough, separated
- Sesame seed

Preheat oven to 425°F. Grease a 2-quart casserole; set aside. Combine cornstarch, onion, bouillon, basil, and salt in large saucepan. Stir in tomatoes with liquid, carrots, and Worcestershire. Cook and stir until thickened. Add Kielbasa, potatoes, celery, and parsley; heat until bubbly. Turn mixture into prepared casserole. Quickly arrange biscuits on top with sides touching. Sprinkle on sesame seed. Bake for 12 to 15 minutes, or until biscuits are golden brown.

Smoked sausage links or frankfurters can be substituted for the Kielbasa, if desired.

Potato Cheese Casserole ———— 10 servings

- 1 package (32 ounces) frozen Southern-style hashed brown potatoes
- 1 cup dairy sour cream
- 1 cup shredded Cheddar cheese
- 2 cans (10 3/4 ounces each) cream of potato soup, undiluted
- 1/4 cup grated Parmesan cheese

Preheat oven to 300°F. Butter a 9 × 13-inch baking dish; set aside. Combine all ingredients, except Parmesan cheese, in large bowl. Turn mixture into prepared baking dish. Sprinkle Parmesan cheese evenly over top. Bake 1 1/2 hours.

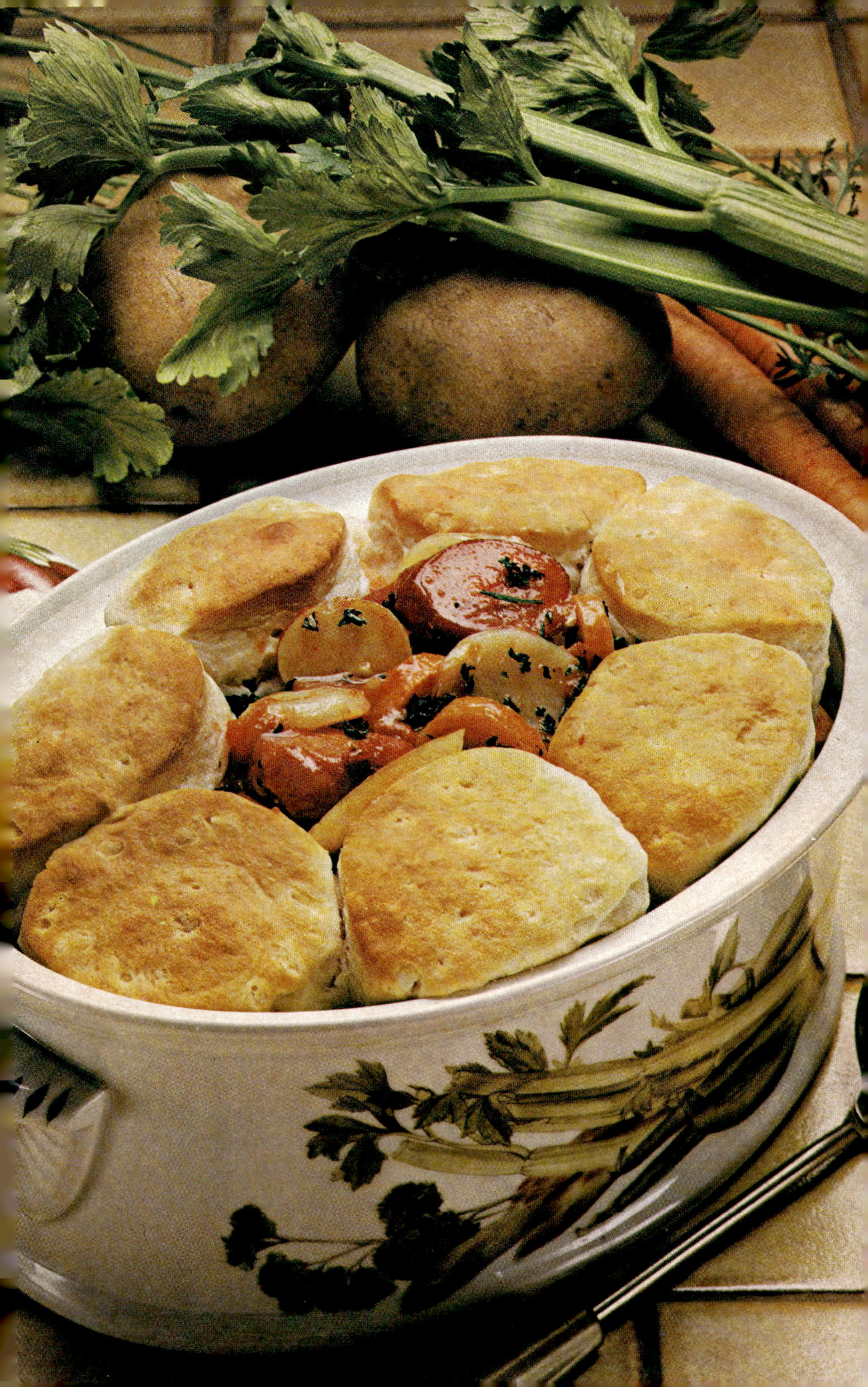

Baked Brunch Eggs — 12 servings

- 2 tablespoons butter or margarine
- 1 package (32 ounces) frozen Southern-style hashed brown potatoes
- 3 tablespoons chopped onion
- 15 eggs, slightly beaten
- 1 cup half-and-half
- 1 teaspoon salt
- 1/4 teaspoon pepper
- 1 teaspoon prepared mustard
- 1 cup shredded Cheddar cheese

Preheat oven to 350°F. Melt butter in large skillet. Add potatoes and onion; fry until potatoes are tender and golden brown. Spoon into 9×13-inch baking dish. Combine eggs, half-and-half, salt, pepper, and mustard in large bowl. Pour over potatoes. Bake 45 minutes. Sprinkle with cheese. Return to oven until cheese is melted.

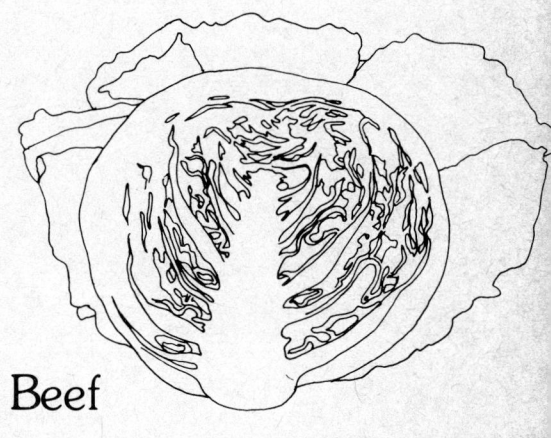

Quick Corned Beef and Cabbage — 4 to 6 servings

- 4 tablespoons butter or margarine
- 3 cups coarsely shredded cabbage
- 1 package (6 ounces) hashed brown potatoes with onion
- 1 teaspoon Worcestershire sauce
- 1/2 teaspoon salt
- 2 cups cut up cooked corned beef
- 1 teaspoon caraway seed (optional)

Melt butter in 10-inch skillet. Stir in cabbage, potatoes, 1 1/2 cups water, Worcestershire, and salt. Cook on moderate heat 17 to 20 minutes, or until liquid is absorbed and bottom is browned. Add corned beef and caraway seed. Turn potatoes with spatula. Cook until corned beef is heated through.

Pantry Potato Salad ──────── 4 to 6 servings

- 2 cans (16 ounces each) sliced potatoes, drained
- 1 can (8 ounces) small green peas, drained
- 1 cup sliced celery
- 1/4 cup sliced green onion
- 3 hard-cooked eggs, sliced
- 1/4 cup sliced stuffed olives
- 1 cup mayonnaise
- 2 teaspoons prepared mustard
- Paprika

Combine potatoes, peas, celery, onion, eggs, and olives in large bowl. Blend mayonnaise and mustard in small bowl. Add to potato mixture; toss to coat. Spoon into serving dish. Sprinkle on paprika.

Easy Hot Potato Salad ──────── 4 servings

- 1 package (5.25 ounces) scalloped potatoes
- 2 tablespoons tarragon-flavored wine vinegar
- 1/3 cup thinly sliced green onions
- 1/4 cup minced green pepper
- 2 teaspoons prepared mustard
- 1/2 teaspoon sugar
- 2 hard-cooked eggs, quartered
- Bacon-flavored bits

Place potato slices in 9-inch skillet. Sprinkle sauce mix over slices. Stir in 3 cups water. Heat to a boil, stirring occasionally. Cover and simmer about 25 minutes, or until potatoes are tender. Stir in vinegar, onions, green pepper, mustard, and sugar; heat through. Garnish with quartered eggs and bacon-flavored bits.

Quick Hamburger au Gratin ──────── 4 servings

- 1 pound lean ground beef
- 1 small onion, chopped
- 1 package (5.5 ounces) au gratin potatoes
- 1/4 teaspoon salt

Brown beef and onion in skillet on moderate heat, stirring occasionally to break up beef; drain fat. Add potatoes and salt to ground beef. Sprinkle sauce mix on top. Stir in water and milk, according to package directions. Bring to a boil, stirring occasionally. Cover and simmer 30 to 35 minutes, or until potatoes are tender.

Garden Potatoes — 3 to 4 servings

- 1 can (16 ounces) whole potatoes, undrained
- 1/4 cup peeled, chopped cucumber
- 2 tablespoons minced green pepper
- 3 medium radishes, thinly sliced
- 2 tablespoons sliced green onions
- 1 tablespoon minced parsley
- 1/2 teaspoon salt
- 1/2 cup dairy sour cream

Heat potatoes in 1-quart saucepan; drain; set aside and keep hot. Combine cucumber, green pepper, radishes, onions, parsley, and salt in small saucepan. Stir in sour cream. Cook on low heat, stirring constantly, until heated through; do not boil. Pour mixture over hot potatoes; stir to coat.

Quick Potato Cheese Soup — 4 servings

- 2 tablespoons onion flakes
- 2 chicken bouillon cubes
- 1/4 teaspoon garlic powder
- 1 1/4 cups potato flakes
- 1 1/2 cups milk
- 1 teaspoon Worcestershire sauce
- 1 cup shredded Cheddar cheese
- 4 slices, bacon, fried and crumbled
- 2 tablespoons minced parsley

Combine 2 1/2 cups water, onion flakes, bouillon, and garlic powder in saucepan. Bring to a boil; simmer 5 minutes, or until bouillon is dissolved. Stir in potato flakes. Slowly stir in milk. Add Worcestershire, cheese, and bacon. Cook on low heat, stirring constantly, until cheese is melted; do not boil. Garnish each serving with parsley. Serve hot.

Encore!

"What do you want me to do with these leftover potatoes?" "Throw them out." "But there are too many to waste. Can't you use them for something?"

We're certain that this conversation takes place often in kitchens throughout the country. This chapter makes use of those potatoes. Whether leftovers or planovers, the end of this act is sure to be followed by calls for "Encore!"

Leftover Potato Hash — 4 servings

- 3 cups chopped leftover cooked potatoes
- 2 cups chopped cooked corned beef
- 6 tablespoons minced onion
- 1/2 teaspoon salt
- Dash fresh pepper
- 1/3 cup half-and-half
- 2 tablespoons vegetable oil

Combine potatoes, corned beef, onion, salt, pepper, and half-and-half in large bowl. Heat oil in large, heavy skillet, spreading over bottom of pan. Spread potato mixture over bottom of skillet. Cook on low heat, without stirring, about 30 minutes, or until light brown on bottom. Using a spatula, loosen bottom of one half of hash. Cut hash in half with spatula; bring loosened side up over other half. Loosen lower half. Tip skillet to slide hash onto serving platter. Serve with chili sauce, or horseradish.

Roast beef or lamb can be substituted for corned beef. For brunch, serve a poached egg on individual portions of hash.

Shepherd's Pie — 2 servings

- 1 cup leftover mashed potatoes
- 3/4 cup cubed cooked roast beef
- 1 cup frozen mixed vegetables, thawed
- 2 tablespoons chopped onion
- 1/2 cup beef gravy, divided
- 2 tablespoons grated Parmesan cheese
- 2 tablespoons minced parsley

Preheat oven to 350°F. Grease 2 small casseroles. Divide mashed potatoes into prepared casseroles. Spread evenly over bottom and sides. Combine beef, vegetables, and onion in small bowl; mix lightly. Spoon over potatoes. Top each with half of the gravy. Sprinkle with Parmesan cheese and parsley. Bake 20 minutes, or until heated through.

To prepare this recipe in microwave oven, place 1 teaspoon butter and onion in 1-cup glass measure. Cook on High 1 minute, or until transparent. Combine ingredients as directed above, using individual approved microwave casseroles. Cover with waxed paper. Cook on High 5 to 6 minutes, or until heated through.

Fluffy Potato Casserole — 4 servings

- 2 cups leftover mashed potatoes
- 1 package (8 ounces) cream cheese, softened
- 1 small onion, finely chopped
- 2 eggs, slightly beaten
- 2 tablespoons all-purpose flour
- 1/4 teaspoon salt
- Dash pepper
- 1 can (3 1/2 ounces) French-fried onion rings

Preheat oven to 300°F. Butter a 1 3/4-quart baking dish; set aside. Combine potatoes, cream cheese, onion, eggs, flour, salt, and pepper in large bowl. Beat with electric mixer until light and fluffy. Spoon into prepared baking dish; sprinkle onion rings on top. Bake, uncovered, 35 minutes, or until heated through.

This dish can be prepared ahead and refrigerated. Add onion rings just before baking. If refrigerated, allow 5 minutes additional baking time.

Baked Squash Puff ———————— 4 servings

1 1/2 cups leftover mashed potatoes
1 package (12 ounces) frozen cooked squash, thawed
2 tablespoons butter or margarine
2 tablespoons onion flakes
1 egg, well beaten
1/2 teaspoon salt
1/8 teaspoon pepper

Preheat oven to 400°F. Grease a 1-quart casserole; set aside. Combine all ingredients in medium bowl; blend well. Spoon into prepared casseole. Bake, uncovered, 30 minutes, or until lightly browned and heated through.

Potatoes in Cream ———————— 6 servings

4 cups diced leftover cooked potatoes
2 cups half-and-half or cream
1/4 cup butter or margarine, cut up
1/2 teaspoon salt
1/2 teaspoon onion salt
1/8 teaspoon pepper

Combine all ingredients in heavy, 10-inch skillet. Cook over low heat 10 minutes, or until sauce is slightly thickened and potatoes are hot, stirring occasionally. To serve, pour into warmed serving dish.

Oyster-Shrimp Chowder ———————— 4 servings

1 can (10 1/2 ounces) oyster stew, undiluted
1 can (10 3/4 ounces) cream of shrimp soup, undiluted
2 medium leftover boiled or baked potatoes, peeled and diced
2 tablespoons minced parsley

Combine stew, cream of shrimp soup, and 2 cups water in 2-quart saucepan. Stir in potatoes and parsley. Heat through; do not boil.

Swiss Potato Kugel ──────── 8 to 10 servings

- 2 tablespoons butter or margarine
- 1 cup finely chopped onions
- 4 cups leftover potatoes, diced or shredded
- 1/2 pound Swiss cheese, shredded
- 1/4 cup flour
- 1 teaspoon salt
- 1/4 teaspoon white pepper
- 3 eggs, slightly beaten
- 3/4 cup half-and-half

Preheat oven to 350°F. Melt butter in large skillet. Sauté onions until limp. Add potatoes, cheese, flour, salt, and pepper; blend well. Combine eggs and half-and-half in small bowl; blend well. Add to potato mixture; blend well. Spoon mixture into 9-inch square baking dish. Bake 20 to 30 minutes, or until golden brown. Cool 5 minutes. Cut into squares.

Potato Croquettes ──────── 6 servings

- 2 cups leftover mashed potatoes
- 2 tablespoons minced onion
- 1 egg, slightly beaten
- 1 tablespoon grated Parmesan cheese
- 2 tablespoons minced parsley
- 3/4 cup fine dry bread crumbs
- 2 tablespoons vegetable oil

Combine potato, onion, egg, cheese, and parsley in medium bowl; blend thoroughly. Shape into 6 croquettes. Spread bread crumbs on waxed paper or in pie plate. Dip croquettes in crumbs, turning to coat evenly; set aside. Heat vegetable oil in large skillet on moderate heat. Place croquettes in hot oil; cook about 4 minutes, or until brown on each side. Serve hot.

---

1 tablespoon minced green pepper can be added to potato mixture, if desired.

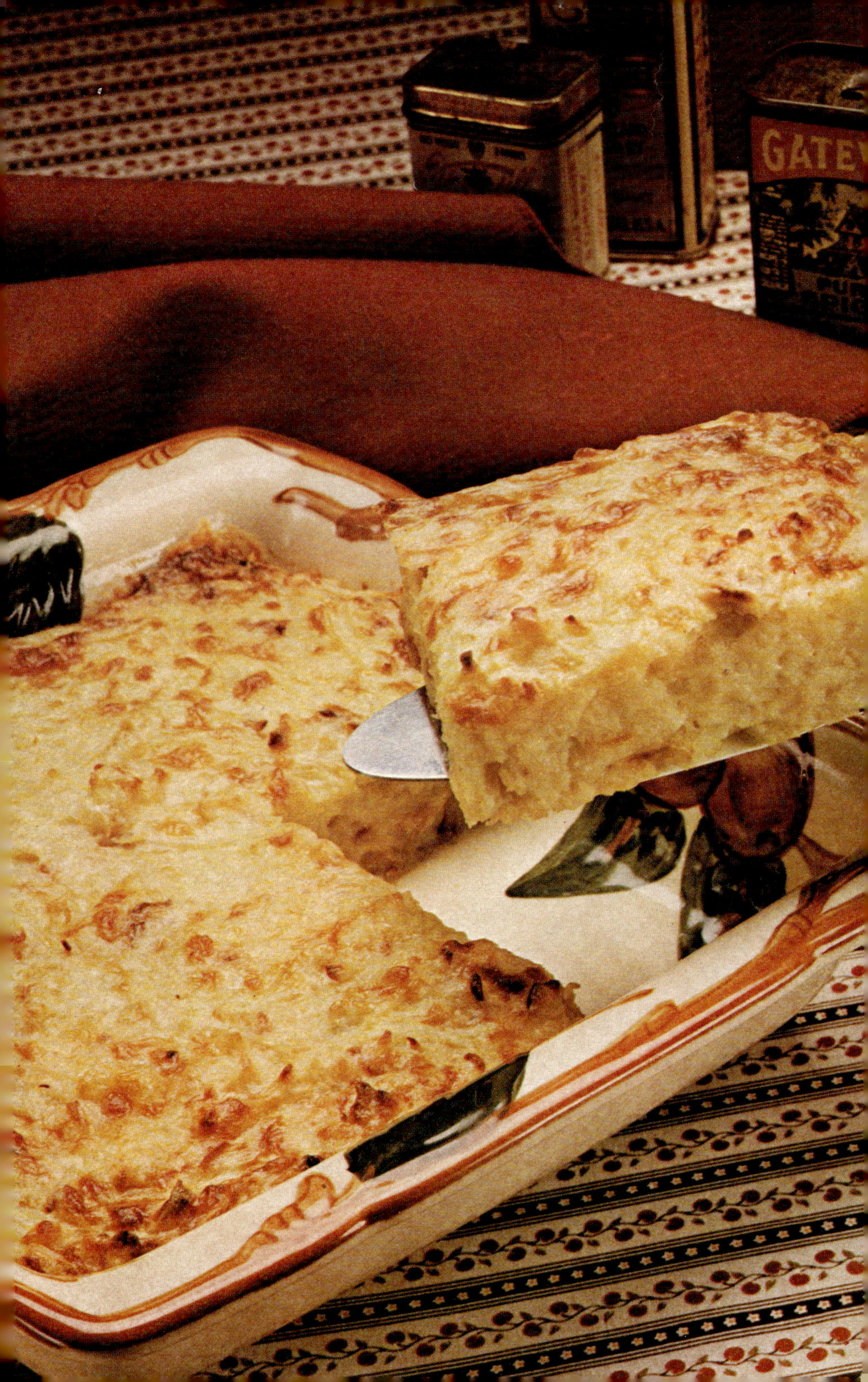

Salmon Potato Patties ———— 6 servings

- 2 leftover baked potatoes
- 1 egg, slightly beaten
- 1 tablespoon onion flakes
- 1 tablespoon minced parsley
- 1 teaspoon celery seed
- 1 can (15 1/2 ounces) pink salmon, drained, skin and bones removed, and flaked
- 1 cup crushed corn flakes
- 3 tablespoons butter or margarine

Peel and rice potatoes. Combine potatoes, egg, onion, parsley, celery seed, and salmon in large bowl; blend well. Chill thoroughly. Shape into 6 patties. Dip both sides of patties in corn flakes to coat. Melt butter in large skillet. Carefully sauté patties on both sides until brown. Serve hot.

Serve with sauce made of heated cream of celery soup and 1/2 soup can milk, if desired.

Pigs in Potato Blanket ———— 4 servings

- 2 cups leftover mashed potatoes
- 1 teaspoon minced onion
- 1 teaspoon minced parsley
- 1 egg yolk
- 1 egg
- 1 tablespoon milk
- 8 fully-cooked small sausages or Vienna sausages
- 2/3 cup fine dry bread crumbs
- Peanut or corn oil for deep-fat frying

Combine potatoes, onion, parsley, and egg yolk in small bowl; blend thoroughly; set aside. Combine egg and milk in separate bowl; blend well; set aside. Press about 1/4 cup potato mixture around each sausage; roll in crumbs, then in egg mixture and again in crumbs; set aside. Heat oil in deep-fat fryer or large saucepan to 375°F. Deep-fat fry sausages until golden brown. Serve hot.

INDEX

Almond(s)
  Bars, 139
  Chocolate Torte, 140
American Fries, 20
Appetizers, 23-32
Apple(s)
  Potato Chip Apple Crisp, 142
  Potato Salad, 47
Applesauce Potato Bread, 105
Apricot filling for Potato Kolache, 103
Aunt Gypsy's Doughnuts, 109
Autumn Soup, 40

Babka, 119
Bacon
  Baked Potatoes-Bacon-Eggs, 85
  Potato, Cheese and Bacon Casserole, 59
  and Potato Puff, 59
  Tater Bits, 32
Baked potatoes
  -Bacon-Eggs, 85
  Basic, 14
  Boston, 78
  Halves, 74
  Twice-, 17
Baked Squash Puff, 153
Basic Baked Potatoes, 14
Beans
  Lamb and Lima Stew, 62
  Senate, and Potato Soup, 39
Beef
  Creamed Chipped, 86
  French Beef Ragout, 120
  Golden Creamy Chipped, 90
  Hearty Beef Stew, 53
  Hot, on a Tater, 93
  Mushroom-Beef and Duchess Potatoes, 53
  Quick Corned, and Cabbage, 148

  Stroganoff, 88
  See also Hamburger
Bigos, 127
Boiled Potatoes, 15
Boston Baked Potatoes, 78
Bran muffins, Crunchy, 98
Bread
  Country Rye, 112
  Torte, 139
  See also Potato bread
Broccoli-Ham Sling, 88
Browned Potatoes in Cream, 145

Cabbage
  Calico Salad, 45
  Caloric content of potatoes, 9-10
  Kraut and Potato Casserole, 56
  Quick Corned Beef and, 148
Caramel Frosting, 100
Carbohydrate content of potatoes, 11
Cauliflower
  -Potato Purée, 68
  -Potato Soup, 34
Cheddar, Chili- Topping, 90
Cheese
  Chili-Cheddar Topping, 90
  as filling for Potato Kolache, 102
  Potato, Cheese and Bacon Casserole, 59
  Potato Cheese Casserole, 146
  Quick Potato Cheese Soup, 150
  in Twice-Baked Potatoes, 17
Cherry(ies)
  Cheesecake, 107
  Potato Cherry Nut Loaf, 104
Chicken
  Fricassee, 62-63
  Grandma's Chicken Pie, 63
  à la King, 95

157

Chili-Cheddar Topping, 90
Chips
  Game, 21
  Tiffany, 25
  See also Potato chip(s)
Chocolate
  Almond Chocolate Torte, 140
  Covered Potato Candy, 132
  Frosting, 107
  Potato Drop Cookies, 138
  Slim Chocolate Cake, 106
  Spicy Cocoa Cookies, 137
Cinnamon Twist Coffee Cake, 112-113
Clam-Potato Pie, 65
Classic Potato Cake, 106
Coconut Chip Cookies, 137
Coconut Pecan Balls, 131
Cookies and candies, 131-139
Cornish Pasty, 124
Cottage Fries, 22
Country Rye Bread, 112
Country Stew, 50
Country-Style Potato Pancakes, 71
Cream of Potato Soup, 38
Creamed Chipped Beef, 86
Creamed Ham and Peas, 93
Creamed Potatoes, 82
Creamy Dutch Potatoes, 129
Creamy Frosting, 108
Creamy Paprika Potatoes, 84
Creamy Potato Salad, 47
Crispy Pecan Cookies, 136
Crunchy Bran Muffins, 98
Crustless Tuna-Potato Quiche, 65

Danish Glazed Potatoes, 120
Delmonico Potatoes, 79
Dollar Potatoes, 80
Doughnuts
  Aunt Gypsy's, 109
  Jelly-Filled Drop, 109
  Raised Potato, 108
Dutchess Potatoes, 75

Easy Hot Potato Salad, 149
Eggs
  Baked Brunch, 148
  Baked Potatoes-Bacon-Eggs, 85
  Italian Omelet, 128
Equivalents and substitutions, 8-9

Fiber content of potatoes, 11
Fish
  and Mushroom Ragout, 66
  -Potato Chowder, 36
  Savory, 87
  Seafood Thermidor, 95
  See also Salmon; Shrimp; Tuna
Flemish Pork, 122
Fluffy Apple-Potato Pancakes, 78
Fluffy Potato Casserole, 152
Frankfurter Wonder, 60
Freezing potatoes, 7-8
French Beef Ragout, 120
French Fries, 20
French Potato Salad, 46
Fries,
  American, 20
  Cottage, 22
  French, 20
  Steakhouse, 15

Game Chips, 21
Garden Potatoes, 150
Garlic-Parsley Potato Balls, 145
German Potato Salad, 41
Gnocci, 130
Golden Creamy Chipped Beef, 90
Grandma's Chicken Pie, 63
Guacamole Topping, 89

Ham
  Broccoli-Ham Sling, 88
  Creamed, and Peas, 93
  Party, and Potato Salad, 48
  and Potato Chowder, 33
  and Potato Quiche, 31
  and Potatoes au Gratin, 58
Hamburger
  Casserole, 55
  Pie, 144
  Quick, au Gratin, 149
  Tater-Hamburger Casserole, 145
Harvesting potatoes, 6-7
Hash Browns, 18
Hawaiian Tidbits, 25
Hearty Beef Stew, 53
Heidelberg Casserole, 73
History of potatoes, 5-6
Honey Whole Wheat Bread, 114-115
Hot Beef on a Tater, 93
Hot German Potato Supper, 144

Irish Prairie Oaten, 123

Knockwurst Potato Salad, 44
Kraut and Potato Casserole, 56

Lamb and Lima Stew, 62
Leftover Potato Hash, 151
Lemon Potato Bread, 115
Lemony Tuna and Mashed Potatoes, 64
Liver Sausage and Potato Ring, 23
Lunch Patties, 52
Long Whites, 6-7
Low-calorie accompaniments for potatoes, 9

Madison Avenue Potato Salad, 44
Mashed Potato(es), 13
   Casserole, 84
   Lemony Tuna and, 64
   Spice Cake, 104
Meat and poultry, 49-64
   See also Beef; Pork; Chicken; Turkey
Milan Potato Mold, 117
Minerals and vitamin content of potatoes, 11
Mock Sour Cream, 80
Moussaka, 123
Mushroom(s)
   -Beef and Duchess Potatoes, 53
   Fish and, Ragout, 66
   Shrimp-Mushroom Topper, 92
   and Wine Topper, 87

Nacho Rounds, 26
Nicoise Salad, 42
Northern Italian Meat Sauce, 92
Nutritive value of potatoes, 9-11

Old-Fashioned Creamed Turkey, 96
One-Dish Deluxe, 50
Onion(s)
   -Potato Bake, 73
   Steak, and Potato Pie, 55
Orange Potato Bread, 113
Oriental Dip, 24
Oyster-Shrimp Chowder, 153

Pantry Potato Salad, 149
Parsley
   Garlic-Parsley Potato Balls, 145
   Parslied Small Potatoes, 16

Party Ham and Potato Salad, 48
Party Potatoes, 79
Patrician Potatoes, 72
Peas
   Creamed Ham and, 93
   Vegetable Split Pea Soup, 38
Peppers, Potato Stuffed, 60
Pigs in Potato Blanket, 156
Pork
   Flemish, 122
   Pigs in Potato Blanket, 156
   Roast, with Potatoes, 57
   See also Ham
Potato(es)
   Anna, 75
   Bar, 80
   Basil, 76
   -Broccoli Bake, 74
   -Celery Casserole, 81
   Cheese and Bacon Casserole, 59
   Cheese Casserole, 146
   Cherry Nut Loaf, 104
   Chowder, 34
   Cinnamon Rolls, 103
   -Coconut Bar Roll, 133
   in Cream, 153
   Croquettes, 154
   Crust, 141
   Drop Biscuits, 97
   Dumplings, 82
   on the Grill, 72
   Honey Dips, 116
   Ice Box Rolls, 99
   Knishes, 128
   Kolache, 102
   Kugel, 121
   and Meatball Casserole, 56
   Minestrone Soup, 35
   Nests, 136
   Paprika with Smoked Sausage, 58
   Pasta, 69
   -Peanut Butter Roll, 132
   Puffs, 21
   Roll-Ups, 111
   Salad Romano, 45
   Soufflé, 67
   Stuffed Peppers, 60
   Stuffing, 71
   -Tomato Bisque, 36
   -Tuna Chowder, 39
   Waffles, 99

Potato bread(s), 114
  Applesauce, 105
  Cordon Bleu, 32
  Sticks, 111
Potato chip(s), 18
  Apple Crisp, 142
  Cookies, 133
  Game, 21
  Tiffany, 25
Potato peels
  Spicy, 24
  Tangy, 26
  Twice-Baked Potato Skins, 24
Prune filling for Potato Kolache, 102
Pumpkin-Potato Soup, 35

Quick Corned Beef and Cabbage, 148
Quick Hamburger au Gratin, 149
Quick Potato Cheese Soup, 150
Quick Potato Coffee Cake, 105
Quick Sausage-Vegie Stew, 146

Raised Potato Doughnuts, 108
Raisin Drop Cookies, 138
Red Flannel Hash, 49
Riced Potatoes, 22
Roast Pork with Potatoes, 57
Roasted Potato Fans, 15
Roesti, 127
Round Reds, 6-7
Round Whites, 6-7
Russet, 6-7
Russian Borscht, 126

Salads, 40-48
Salisbury Skillet Supper, 143
Salmon
  Potato Patties, 156
  Potato Salad, 41
Sausage
  Knockwurst Potato Salad, 44
  Potato Paprika with Smoked, 58
  Quick Sausage-Vegie Stew, 146
Savory Fish, 87
Scalloped Potatoes, 81
Scottish Scones, 129
Seafood Thermidor, 95
Senate Bean and Potato Soup, 39
Shepherd's Pie, 152
Shoestring Potatoes, 21
Squash
  Baked Squash Puff, 153

Shrimp
  Mushroom Topper, 92
  Oyster-Shrimp Chowder, 153
Skillet Supper Salad, 40
Slim Chocolate Cake, 106
Soft Potato Pretzels, 135
Soups, 33-40
South-of-the-Border Topping, 86
Spaghetti Supreme, 89
Spanish Potatoes, 122
Spicy Cocoa Cookies, 137
Spicy Potato Peels, 24
Spinach
  Pasta, 68
  Spud Supreme, 96
Spudzagna, 52
Steakhouse Fries, 15
Steamed Potatoes, 16
Storage of potatoes, 7
Substitutions and equivalents, 8-9
Superb Garden Salad, 46
Swiss Potato Kugel, 154

Tangy Crisp Potato Peels, 26
Tater-Hamburger Casserole, 145
Tex-Mex Green Chili Stew, 121
Tiffany Chips, 25
Tomato, Potato- Bisque, 36
Tomato Sauce, Zucchini and, 94
Tuna
  Crustless Tuna-Potato Quiche, 65
  Lemony, and Mashed Potatoes, 64
  Potato-Tuna Chowder, 39
  Topper, 94
Turkey, Old-Fashioned Creamed, 96
Twice-Baked Potato Skins, 24
Twice-Baked Potatoes, 17

Vegetable(s)
  Dip, 25
  Split Pea Soup, 38
Versatility of potatoes, 6
Vichyssoise, 126
Vitamin and mineral content of potatoes, 11

Whipped Cream Potato Torte, 141
Wine
  Mushroom and Wine Topper, 87
  Potatoes, 69
  Wisconsin Spice Cake, 100

Zucchini and Tomato Sauce, 94